GOLF

LEARN FROM THE LEGENDS

GOLF

LEARN FROM THE LEGENDS

Bob Mullen
Illustrations by Tom Weyl

Golf: Learn from the Legends

Printed in the United States of America
Printed on acid-free paper

Library of Congress Control Number: 2019940473
AR Publications, Pinole, California

ISBN-13: 978-0-578-49711-2

Cover designed by Wendy Mullen Ruel

To my dad, Earl, and his two younger brothers, Dick and Bob, three men who have loved the game of golf nearly as much as I do. And to my brother Dick, whom I will always miss—on and off the course.

It is also my hope that this book will provide new insight to learning and playing the "most difficult game."

Contents

Contents

Illustrations

Foreword

Who dares to teach must never cease to learn.
—John Cotton Dana

When Bob Mullen, a United States Golf Teachers Federation (USGTF) master teacher and examiner, came to me in 2009 and asked me to write the foreword to his book, *Golf from the Ground Up*, I asked him why he was writing the book. His response was that he had something new and useful to write about. He called it the "platform." After a review of his book, I agreed that his was an instruction book with a new angle on learning the fundamentals of the game of golf. Eighty-four percent of the customer reviews on Amazon were five stars, indicating that those who purchased the book were not disappointed in what he had to contribute to teaching the game of golf.

The USGTF family includes eighteen thousand teachers, and Bob is one of 475 who, through expanding their knowledge and understanding of the game, have reached the level of master teacher. Since writing his first book, Bob has followed not only the letter but the meaning expressed by Dana's quote, which has become part of the USGTF principles. What he learned is the reason for his second book.

Bob explained to me that in 1975, according to a study by *Golf Digest*, the score of the average golfer was around one hundred. Sam Snead looked at that number and wrote, "Something's wrong somewhere."[1] This statement became the focus of Snead's golf instruction book, *Sam Snead Teaches You His Simple "Key" Approach to Golf*. Snead's belief was that the substantial improvement in equipment and course maintenance should have led to lower overall scores, but it hadn't. The intent of Snead's book was to explain the fundamentals of golf in such a way that every golfer would improve. Nine years earlier Bobby Jones wrote this opinion of golf instruction: "It seems to me that writing about the golf swing has become too technical and complicated, and even the most earnest teaching professional presents the game to his pupil as far more complicated than it really is."[2] In the last fifty years, millions and millions of words have been written describing in detail how to play the game. It is safe to say that all this advice is very similar—some of it good and some bad.

It is now 2018, even more equipment improvements have been made, and golf courses pride themselves in their immaculate condition. Golf should be easier to play, and lower scores should result. But the average score for a male golfer, as published by the United States Golf Association in 2017, remains at one hundred. USGTF studies have shown that four years after a golfer establishes his or her handicap, the golfer reaches a plateau and makes little further improvement. The handicap remains stagnant. Bob explains that golf is an experience sport. Learning takes place either explicitly from lessons, books, and videos, or it occurs implicitly through exposure to success and failure or through observation of other golfers, and this learning must follow an orderly path.

The continuing high golf scores, in spite of great improvements in equipment and courses, and the challenges inherent in learning and improving skills in this difficult sport became the motivation for Bob's second book. Something is still wrong somewhere.

I believe a good golf book will include four things: first, what you need to learn (the fundamentals and the swing); second, explanations that lead to student learning; third, illustrations that accurately depict the actions; and fourth, and most important, a teaching foundation that allows the student to develop confidence in what he or she has learned. The more we learn about the game and the people who play it, the more we understand that the key to successful golf lies in the self-confidence of the player. How does Bob address this important element?

Bob felt that the answer was hiding in plain sight and remained there for years waiting to be discovered. Smarter men than he had failed in this effort, so he sought advice from one of the greatest problem solvers of all time. In the writings of Albert Einstein, he found his answer. He then knew that he had to "step off the tee box" and look at the problem from a different perspective.

Oddly enough, Bob's book begins on the Marine Corps rifle range at Quantico. He blends that story of Marine Corps ethos with a discussion of trust. The discussion of trust leads to self-confidence. He then gives us a brief but informative section on understanding the game and introduces seven historic golf teacher-players he calls the Legends, whose writings become the book's backbone. This is what editors would call a really good read.

The real meat of the matter is the simple-to-understand and all-important discussion of how the human brain learns motor skills. The action required to strike the golf ball is complex, but through repetition the golfer develops a swing. Learning the swing and associated motor skills is not based on muscle memory, but on brain function. Bob writes that learning any motor skill requires making changes in two areas of the brain: first, the memory of the action is held by the frontal cortex; second, that memory produces neuron changes in the motor cortex. No permanent learning of motor skills—changes in the motor cortex—can occur without repeated physical action; this is called practice. Once the golfer understands this process, he or she will know that no amount of verbal explanation or study alone will improve performance.

Bob explained to me that deciding what to teach was relatively easy. The fundamentals of golf have changed very little since Bobby Jones wrote his five hundred thousand words and made his movies. Golfers may have physically changed over the years—they have become bigger, stronger, faster—but the laws of physics and human physical limitations guide the processes used to strike a golf ball. Those basic laws can't change. As a teacher-golfer and writer, Bob explained it was not his job to impress readers with his knowledge or ability to play the game. It is his job to give them the tools and confidence they need to play the best game of golf they can play. The tools come from the Legends, and the self-confidence comes from trusting what these acknowledged experts teach.

This book includes the excellent, pencil-drawn illustrations by Tom Weyl. These illustrations add significantly to the book as a teaching tool as well as providing beautiful representations of the game we love. I have learned that signed reproductions of some of these illustrations will be made available through the publisher.

Learning the fundamentals is just the first step. To successfully strike a ball repeatedly, the skills have to be performed under pressure, and this is where confidence leads the way. There is a connection between learning a skill, trusting in that skill, and having the confidence to perform. To perform under pressure, we have to believe in the source of our information. To give us confidence in what we are learning, this easy-to-understand instruction book is based on the teachings of seven Legends: Bobby Jones, Ben Hogan, Sam Snead, Harvey Penick, Arnold Palmer, Jack Nicklaus, and Tom Watson. When these are our instructors, we have every reason to trust what we have learned.

Geoff Bryant, President
United States Golf Teachers Federation

Preface

I remember it like it was yesterday. The range flags were fluttering. A steady breeze was blowing from right to left. I had to adjust my sights for yardage and the wind and keep my first shot in at least the four-point circle so I could still qualify as an expert. It seemed like an impossible task. I could afford only one shot in the four ring; the rest had to be bull's-eyes, or I was dead. At that point, I had to rely on what I had been taught by the Marine Corps instructors. I had to trust the fundamentals—the training that had prepared me well for this moment. I was ready; I simply had to trust what I knew. I had to stop catastrophizing and clear my mind. I had to make my sight adjustments, prepare correctly, relax, and above all else stop thinking about the details to allow myself to shoot exactly as I had countless times in training.

Fast forward to my office with every surface piled high with books by the best golfers who ever played or taught the game. I had written so many beginnings to my new golf-teaching book, and the waste basket was full of those efforts. Finally, after months of writing and rewriting, it all fell into place....

Something's wrong somewhere.
—Sam Snead

In 2009, I wrote a golf instruction book titled *Golf from the Ground Up*. It was well received, and I was happy with the results, but as an instruction book it did not achieve what I had hoped it would. I needed to understand why. Ten years have passed, and during those intervening years, I have come to understand more about the teaching and learning of motor skills for adult learners. Since I see myself primarily as an educator, I am now able to offer a more meaningful new book.

Over the years, I have read and reread the books of my favorite golf pros to whom I have come to refer as the seven Legends. It was in 1975 when one of them, Sam Snead, saw a problem and wrote about it. The average golfer was scoring one hundred despite what Snead considered to be major improvements in equipment and playing conditions. He described a game that he believed had gotten remarkably easier to play. They now had a pitching wedge, a sand wedge, metal shafts, and what he described as the modern driver. The greens now putted true and did not have weeds and worm casts. The golf courses of today are vastly improved compared to those in Snead's time. Club technology is now what can be described as space age, and yet forty years later the National Golf Foundation reports the average male golfer still scores one hundred. There has been no change in the average male golfer's score.

Believing that a lot of instruction came "out of the rare air...and really contributes little or nothing useful to the game of the weekend golfer,"[3] Sam set out to solve the problem of the weekend golfer; his solution was to write a book. The purpose of his book was to simplify instruction using the fundamentals, which would help people learn the game he loved. He was tired of seeing golfers trying to improve their play and not succeeding.

The popularity of the game had grown because of television coverage of the big three—Palmer, Player, and Nicklaus—but he was worried that players were not staying with the game because the way that they were being taught made learning too difficult. He reasoned that if someone could explain the fundamentals in simple, understandable terms, golfers everywhere would soon be striking the ball down the fairway, average scores would drop below one hundred, and America would fall in love with the game of golf. Sam wrote an excellent book, and since that time, the shelves of bookstores have been filled with his books and books written by the other Legends and golfing professionals on how to play golf. All of these books describe the fundamentals necessary to master the game of golf.

Snead was right forty years ago, and he is still right today, when he said, "something's wrong somewhere."[4] When something is wrong, most people go to a problem solver. I know of no better problem solver than Albert Einstein, and, although I am sure he never played a round of golf in his life, he solved problems every day. It was his thinking that helped me out: "No problem can be solved by the same consciousness that created it. We need to see the world anew."

With this idea in mind, I stepped off the tee box so to speak and looked for a solution that hadn't been tried before. The idea for the book began to take form. I had to teach golfers how to learn—but how? After many discussions with my editor about learning, the Marine Corps ethos, confidence, and much of what the seven Legends have said in their books, we realized that the major goal of any golf instruction should be to give the student

Figure P.1 Albert Einstein

Preface

self-confidence. She then left me with this thought: trust is the foundation of self-confidence. What a thought!

"The Golfer" is the first chapter of part I. The game of golf has so many layers, and, like any game, we need to understand both the game and something about those who play it. We must know the ins and outs of golf beyond just hitting the ball. No one—no matter how experienced or how articulate or how successful—can explain the game in one chapter or one book or, for that matter, in one lifetime. It is an experience sport that is constantly changing, and so much of it is learned by doing; the more someone plays, the more he knows.

Also in part I, I introduce the seven Legends who are the sources for some stories and supply the fundamentals for part III. The stories of the Legends and of the average Joe who plays at the public course are endlessly fascinating to those of us who heed the siren song of the game. We know why someone stands in line at four o'clock in the morning to get a tee time for next weekend, calls a penalty on himself for a ball that moved when only he saw it move, and wades in a muddy creek in new golf shoes to get a ball. Explaining our game is an attempt to explain the unexplainable. Much like the narrator in the very old radio drama whose voice intoned "the shadow knows," there are things in golf only the experienced golfer knows. To play any game well, we must understand it, and longtime players and novices alike know that the stories of golfing and golfers, of successes and mishaps, never lose their hold on us. Every conversation connects us to the game long after the last hole is just a memory.

"Learning to Learn" starts off part II and is a new and unusual topic for a golf book. It is the reason for this book. We can't go on teaching and preaching the fundamentals and expecting students to try to learn golf while ignoring the key question implicit in Snead's statement: Why aren't golfers getting better at the game of golf? Adult learners need to know how adults learn motor skills.

Learning golf is not hard; it is just hard work. It is hard work because playing golf involves many distinct motor skills. Most of these motor skills seem easy to learn, but motor skills are harder to learn for adults. Learning new skills requires practice, and practice requires a schedule. If golfers are willing to discipline themselves to follow the process and build their games on the proven fundamentals, skill by skill, they will come closer to achieving the ultimate goal—a repeatable swing with a predictable result. As we approach that goal, we learn to trust our training and the fundamentals that define our game.

If we understand how our brain works, the road to sound fundamental golf is within our reach. Brain science is no longer a mystery. We know how the neurons work. We know how information travels from sensors in our body to the brain and back to the muscles. We know how long it takes on average for a golfer to learn a motor skill.

The teachers in chapter 2 are seven of the most highly regarded teachers and players who have ever picked up a club. Golfers can trust the lessons in this book because the information comes from the best possible source—no fake news! Trust is the foundation of self-confidence.

I could write fundamentals—I've been perfecting mine for fifty years and teaching for thirty—but that information would come from Bob Mullen. These fundamentals must have standing just like the instructor had standing who taught me to shoot in the Marine Corps. Standing is ethos and ethos creates trust and trust creates self-confidence. The Marines who taught me to shoot had names, but names do not create standing. The fact that they had the reputation of the United States Marine Corps behind them and that they were Marines whose military occupational specialty (MOS) and rank made them specifically qualified to teach other Marines how to shoot gave them standing in the corps. Likewise, the seven professional golfers whose books I have studied for three years have similar standing in the golf world. The seven Legends encompass the ethos of the golf world—not just the how-tos of the fundamentals, but also the highest values of sportsmanship, service to others, and camaraderie.

When I first told my story about qualifying as an expert shooter while in the Marine Corps to my good friend, golfing buddy, and the artist for this book, Tom Weyl, I was ultimately telling a story about self-confidence. Building confidence is certainly a major element of this book, and that is why I am repeating it now. No one can play golf well without self-confidence, just as I could not shoot without self-confidence at one of the most critical and most vulnerable times in my life. I had to believe in what I had been taught, or I would fail. In retrospect, I know that the key to my success that day on the range was very simple; it was my level of self-confidence.

What we learn is useless if we cannot use it when we need it. When I prepared to shoot at those twenty-inch targets more than a quarter mile away, I had total belief in what I had learned. I only had to focus. For a frame of reference, a twenty-inch target is approximately four times the size of this book, and a quarter mile is a long par four—440 yards. To fire that rifle successfully, I had to trust the Marine way—no other thought could be in my head. I had to use the methods and fundamentals demonstrated and taught to me by the Marine Corps instructors. I could have no doubts that what I had learned would make me successful, so I did not deviate from what I had been taught. What I had done in practice I believed I could do again. So, as I set in at the five hundred, I put the previous bad shots behind me—they did not exist—and I believed I could succeed. I shot ten for ten from the five hundred. It was that simple, or perhaps that complicated; I had trusted in the fundamentals, and I succeeded. I was awarded the Marine Rifle Expert badge. The self-confidence came as a by-product of trust in the Marine Corps ethos.

There are naysayers who would challenge the above conclusion. Noted American writer, journalist, satirist, critic, and scholar H. L. Mencken argues, "[T]here is always a well-known solution to every human problem—neat, plausible, and wrong."[5] In response to Mr. Mencken's legendary cynicism, I would respond: The Marine Corps has been, since its inception, the finest fighting force in the world. The Marine ethos is simple to explain. It is summarized in the Marine Corps motto, which is short and to the point: *Semper Fidelis*. Most Marines would just say *Semper Fi* or Always Faithful. These two words have made giants out of mere mortals in combat; legends have appeared not so much because of the strength of the individuals, but because of the unity of the command and the ethos of the corps. The Marines are about trust in themselves and their fellow Marines. That trust comes from this ethos, and that is what makes a Marine a Marine. In their training, they emphasize fundamentals, but more important, because of who they are, there is trust in those fundamentals, and trust is a powerful tool.

I had previously asked myself what the average golfer needs to be successful and to enjoy the game of golf. My answer had always been to trust in the fundamentals.

Self-confidence comes from trust. Golfers need to learn fundamentals from a source they trust and won't stray from the first time they have a crappy day at the course. Confidence erodes easily when shots go off line and putts don't fall. Who or what do we challenge when that happens? Golfers generally blame the fundamentals rather than their execution of the fundamentals. If another golfer tells them to try this or that, they make a change. This takes them on the road to the destruction of whatever game they have.

A good game needs to be built on fundamentals from a source that is battle tested—a source that can be trusted—much like the Marine Corps training. When there is an error or a string of errors—and there will be—we need to look to our training, analyze what fundamental has broken down, and get back to work. There is absolutely no better foundation for our golf game than learning the fundamentals from the seven Legends. In a sense, I have placed myself in the position of scribe for Jones, Snead, Penick, Hogan, Palmer, Nicklaus, and Watson. None of the fundamentals in this book are new, and when the Legends wrote their books, they passed on what they had learned from their instructors, their years of competitive play, and trial and error. This book contains the seven Legends' interpretations of golf's fundamentals.

I have, on more than one occasion, imagined what it would be like to have the seven Legends together discussing the fundamentals. I know full well that each one of them learned his fundamentals through years of practice, through starts and stops, through trial and error, trying out what did work and what didn't until each found his own game—a winning game. Then he wrote about what he had learned individually. What is so amazing is that they all wrote very nearly the same things. Two quotes stick in my mind that seem to sum up the thoughts of the group as a whole.

"When we set side by side the playing methods of the best golfers, we always find that the basic movements and their orderly sequence are the same within a very narrow range."[6] (Bobby Jones)

"For all the personal touches and mannerisms which are part of their individual styles, I have never seen a great player whose method of striking the ball did not include the fundamentals…."[7] (Ben Hogan)

The seven of them may have been playing in different eras and had different instruction from different pros, but when they sat down to write about the fundamentals, their explanations are consistent. They, individually and as a group, agreed that learning the game of golf was a process that required a commitment to practice and a plan. They are, without question, leaders one and all, and men worthy of following into battle. As a former Marine, there is no higher compliment I can give another man.

The body of work produced by these men is huge. The only thing that all of their books lack is the chapter on how to learn. This book offers just that and includes a compilation of the seven Legends' teachings. Champions like Arnold Palmer were eager to share their ideas on how to play the game, and Palmer wrote his first of five instruction books, *My Game and Yours*, in 1983. Bobby Jones wrote more than a half million words in article after article and six books starting in 1961 with *Golf is My Game*; Snead wrote six before he was finished. Perhaps the greatest golfer of all time, Jack Nicklaus, wrote ten, if you include the *Play Better Golf* series. Harvey Penick (not a champion tour golfer, but a renowned instructor) wrote four, and Tom Watson wrote five. Ben Hogan wrote two. The content of their books is centered on the fundamentals of golf, and the central theme is the fact that golf is a game of practice and concentration. No shortcuts are ever mentioned.

The sum of their fundamentals will direct all golfers toward the ability to have a repeatable swing with a predictable ball flight. They would acknowledge that a perfect swing is not a necessity in producing the predicable shot. The most popular instruction book continues to be Ben Hogan's book, *The Five Lessons*. It is the current gold standard as the most popular resource in the golfing world. The value of that book owes as much to the stature of the author as it does to the content. It has great standing because the Hogan name has an aura—a tradition; he is a golfing legend, and readers want to build their game around what Hogan has said. His book has provided many keys to the fundamentals set forth in this book.

It was the great American car manufacturer Henry Ford who said, "Whether you believe you can do a thing or not, you are right." Now it is up to you.

Acknowledgements

To acknowledge every professional and amateur from whom I have learned since my first book would be an impossible task. Everyone who is serious about teaching keeps an open door to learning; it is my goal not only to continue learning, but to always create an environment for the student that is conducive to learning. No teacher worth spending time with talks more than he listens or answers more questions than he asks. I want to thank Geoff Bryant and the USGTF for their support throughout the development and writing of this book.

I also recognize the invaluable help of my golfer friends and beta readers who have given me support, suggestions as they read early manuscripts, and encouragement all the years we have loved this game together. My right hand and best friend, Tom Weyl, the illustrator, made this book possible because of his talent, his knowledge of the game, and his desire to make a contribution to the understanding of how this game is played.

Putting words on paper is easy compared to editing those words, phrases, and paragraphs into a cohesive read. I am indebted to my publisher, Marilyn Huff, and her editor/copyeditor/researcher/magician, Janet Culloton, for their efforts in bringing this book to publication. Having your work rejected is not easy, and these two women are uncompromising in their evaluation of the written word. The result is a good, solid instruction book with the Legends as its backbone and a new look at how we learn motor skills.

Bob Mullen
Spring 2019

Part I

1
The Golfer

Figure 1.1 Uncle Dick and me

The cool morning was a welcome relief from the hot humid days of the Kansas summer. My brother and I had spent the night at my Uncle Dick and Aunt Jodi's house, and they offered two choices for Friday: swimming with Aunt Jodi or golfing with Uncle Dick. My brother was older and got to choose first. I didn't say a word. I had been hitting balls in the cemetery behind our house, and I hoped he would pick swimming. Aunt Jodi won him over by saying that there would be some pretty little girls at the lake. That got him, and I was going to be on a real golf course for the first time in my life.

Uncle Dick was taking me to a public course in Wichita called Clapp Park. I thought I was just going to walk with him while he played. I can remember on the ride to the course when Uncle Dick told me that I would be his caddie. My stomach turned over, and I don't remember much after that until the car stopped in the gravel parking lot. I could barely wait to see the golf course. Uncle Dick pulled his clubs out of the trunk and adjusted the leather strap on his golf bag so I could manage to carry it; we headed for the clubhouse. He told me to wait under this big tree while he went inside, so I stood there with the bag and watched the other golfers.

While I was waiting for him to return, I watched to see how other golfers slung their bags over their shoulders. I tried it a couple of times and had it pretty much figured out by the time Uncle Dick came out the double screen doors. Handing me a stick of Juicy Fruit, he asked if I was ready, and we were off. I put the strap over my shoulder, and, settling the bag across my back, followed him to the first tee. Little did I know then that it was the first page in the first chapter of a story that would last a lifetime.

I was like the young boy who had visions of running off to be in the circus. Uncle Dick had shown me how to hold the club, and he let me hit a couple of balls at Clapp. I wanted to play that game, but had no idea how to make it happen. I had already played plenty of other sports. There was a basketball goal permanently affixed above the garage where I lived, and I practiced regularly with my older brother to ensure my spot on the school teams. A tennis racket and numbered squares painted on the garage wall were my mom's idea for tennis practice. We also took swimming lessons every summer at the park. Fall was synonymous with football at our house, and I have to admit that I really loved that game. There was a high jump pit in the back yard where my brother and I practiced the western roll. As for golf, there was the problem of not having any golf clubs.

One day I was searching my grandpa's side porch where the leftover stuff from my uncles was stashed. As I looked through it all, I occasionally found a useful piece of sports equipment used by some pretty good athletes. Mostly it was old ball gloves and baseball cleats, an old ball cap, or a bat, but nothing I thought was really a treasure. I was ready to give up when I found it—a not-so-worn-out niblick and a few golf balls. I took the club and the balls and headed for our garage. The club was a Rakspin niblick, and it had a wooden shaft. It was rusty, but I cleaned it up and figured I could hit balls with it in the cemetery behind our house. I found an old sock in the rag bag that would hold the seven balls, and I was set to go golfing.

My friend Mary Elizabeth George's dad, who was the caretaker of Maple Grove Cemetery, granted us entry, and inside the cemetery we paid strict adherence to Mr. George's ground rules. I slipped through the opening in the huge hedge that separated our property from the cemetery, and, once on the other side, I had arrived at what was to become my version of a golf course. It was a layout with three targets and no holes. Play began from a patch of grass just inside the hedge to the first target, which was a stubby, gnarled cedar we called the monkey tree. My second target was a mound at the intersection of three roads not far from the base of the monkey tree. The third target was the original patch of grass at the hedge opening. I repeated the triangle over and over again and considered myself a golfer.

I never invited anyone to join me while playing at my course. It was something I did by myself; I enjoyed doing it alone. Besides, I only had seven balls, and a lost ball could not be easily replaced, so I kept a close watch on all seven. There were many long searches after crooked shots ended up in the hedges or on grave sites, but I managed to keep track of the seven balls for most of that summer. My time there was special, but my golf career was temporarily suspended at the end of the summer when I went to work for my dad's construction company.

That summer was more than sixty years ago. President Eisenhower was in office; the country was on the upswing and so was golf. Ike was an avid golfer with a fifteen handicap, and, during the eight years he was in the White House, he reportedly played more than eight hundred rounds of golf. He

Figure 1.2 President Eisenhower

managed to do this while practicing most mornings on a three-thousand-square-foot putting green installed by the United States Golf Foundation with private funds. Ike made a lifetime friend of Arnold Palmer, and their friendship was a major factor in the spread of golf's popularity in the nation. He played often with Bob Hope and General Omar Bradley, and the July 1953 issue of *Golf Digest* stated that Washington, DC, was "seized with golfing fever like never in history." When asked about his game after leaving the White House, President Eisenhower responded, "More people beat me now." It would seem that, at least in the world of golf, rank does have some privileges.

Looking back to the turn of the previous century when William Howard Taft made the first presidential putt, there have been eighteen golfers in the White House with only three of the presidents not being players of the game. Kennedy tried to hide his enjoyment of what he called a Republican sport, but to no avail. Their handicaps have ranged from around twenty to ten, and now with Donald Trump in the White House, we have an exceptional golfer who plays golf on his own courses.

From the most powerful men and women in the world, including the presidents of the United States, to a young boy with a single, well-used club hitting balls on a makeshift course in a cemetery, the game of golf somehow captures imaginations, hearts and, yes, even souls. What is so magical about this game? Some would posit it is the prestige and history of the game that makes it so attractive. I would counter that to the young boy those factors meant nothing as he began his quest, and we only have to look around to see that of the twenty-five million players in the United States today a very large number play in the most casual attire, and I doubt many could pass a simple history exam on the sport. No, it is something much different that draws golfers to the game.

We could say there is some value in the fact that it is the only major competitive sport where anyone can play where the champions play and recreate the shots that champions have made on those exact holes. Golf is a game about the telling and retelling of the beautiful moments and the crushing moments, but most of them belong to someone else. Golf is the only sport that lets the average guy or gal stand where Jones or Hogan or Nicklaus stood on a day and at a time when golfing history was made. Who is likely to forget the day Nicklaus stood 218 yards away from the flag on the seventeenth at Pebble Beach during the final round with a one iron in his hand? Jack was facing a left-to-right cross wind and the pin placement in the right rear of the corner of the green. Golfers today can stand on that tee box and imagine that very shot. The US Open was on the line that day, and most of us would be hoping just to leave it in the bunker close to the green. We would no doubt be reminded of what Lee Trevino said that even God can't hit a one iron, but Jack hit what he described as the best one iron of his life. It bounced once and hit the pin, and he tapped it in for a birdie securing his US Open victory. We could hit balls all day from that spot trying to duplicate Jack's shot and never come close, but in golf any golfer gets the chance to try.

Bob Mullen

The ability to dream is certainly part of golf's allure. Who doesn't arrive at the course thinking that this day might be the day when it all comes together? But that is not why we play the game. There is an even stronger motivation.

I believe it must have something to do with what I read in a book that Bob Cullen wrote called *Why Golf?*. We all have a need to feel competent and in control of our environment, and it is that basic need that calls out to be satisfied. So how does golf fit into this need thing?

A psychiatrist named Joe Silvio explained that a basic psychological need exists, which hitting golf balls satisfies, and Cullen shares it in his book. The need is called the "exploratory-assertive motivational system."[8] Apparently, everyone on the planet has this need. My system satisfies this need when I hit golf balls, and if I don't hit golf balls I am not—like that little dwarf—Happy. Others may satisfy this same need in different ways, but hitting golf balls is the way I get happy, and the more I hit the better I feel.

The discovery of this system involves a story about a blind baby that smiled. In the beginning, no matter what stimulus was tried, the baby did not smile. Researchers tried holding, they tried sounds, they tried touching, and nothing worked. Then one day, when the baby was eight weeks old, bells were hung so the baby's kicking could make them ring. The baby kicked and heard the bells ring, and then the baby smiled. The baby kicked, the bells rang again, and he smiled. In fact, the baby smiled every time his kicking produced the sound of the bells, even though the random ringing of the bells did not produce a smile. It was only when he could manipulate his world—producing the sound of bells ringing—by kicking that made the baby smile. Simply hearing bells ringing did not make him smile. This became one of the bases for the theory behind the exploratory-assertive motivational system. Knowing that we can control our environment gives us each a sense of competence, which induces happiness.

It is the efficacy of the action that is important, not the action itself. For some, the action could be skiing down a mountain slope, shooting a ball through a hoop, knocking down pins on a bowling alley, completing a marathon, or hitting a golf ball. For the golfer, it is his or her action of hitting a ball and making something happen on the course that is pleasing. The proof of that action is fed to the brain by his or her five senses, and it is satisfying. When the senses are stimulated by this manipulation of our environment, we feel good.

Ben Hogan summed it up best when he said, "Perhaps the only true mystery to golf is the essential magnetism the game possesses which makes so many of us, regardless of discouragement, never quite turn in our trench coats and magnifying glasses and stop our search for answers."[9] We are all searching for something, and there are many of us who believe we can find it in the game of golf. It may be learning about golf or it may be what golf teaches us about life or it just may be what golf teaches us about ourselves. Whatever it is, I believe Hogan is right.

Golf brings out something different in everyone who plays. It is not a team sport where unity will help participants play better, and friendliness never earned anyone a par. Golfers are who they are, and it shows up during four hours of play. Four letter words are a part of the golf vernacular,

6

and long and short phrases using words other than duck, poop, and puppy of a female dog are uttered by players of both sexes. Ducking up is not fun, especially if it's just the fourth hole. There is just no pretending that golf doesn't get very frustrating.

Golfers act in unique ways, too. We all have seen a golfer put his foot, and consequently his hundred-dollar golf shoe, in a muddy creek to reach a four-dollar golf ball, but I can guarantee that if that same golfer was asked to go get the groceries out of the car in the pouring rain, he would react as if he had been asked to wade the Mississippi. Most golfers don't like to wake up before dawn on a weekend morning unless, of course, he has a tee time at seven-thirty in the morning that requires a two-hour drive with golfing buddies. And what about the codicil in a golfer's will that requires a cup of his cremated ashes to be saved and ceremoniously spread in the right-hand bunker of the thirteenth hole at exactly midnight on his first birthday following his death? It stipulates that the task is to be carried out by any of his surviving golfing buddies and his nearest surviving relative (which will probably be his wife). The question she will want answered is who in the world wants to drink a shot of Pig's Nose Scotch on a golf course at midnight on that thirteenth hole? My answer: definitely his golfing buddies.

Remember, it is the golfer who will stand six deep in the hot sun to observe a professional who has no chance of winning the tournament go through his routine and hit his shot or attempt a three-foot putt. It is the golfer who plays the game with an ancient putter because he thinks it's lucky. He plays the game in the rain, but doesn't buy an umbrella. He owns winter golf gloves to play in the cold and will invest in colored balls to play in light snow. He believes in eating raw carrots to facilitate playing in near darkness and has worn the same golf hat for three seasons.

Some would say that, considering known golf behaviors, the judgement of the average golfer might be a bit suspect. I challenge that assumption because I know one thing that will send all golfers scurrying to the clubhouse like rats from a sinking ship, and that is lightning. Frostbite and near drowning can be overcome. Anyone can learn to survive a fifty-mile-an-hour wind, and rehydrating can always happen later. But, even knowing the odds of being struck by lightning are set at one in fifteen thousand for an average American, golfers are aware that their odds have been increased exponentially because they carry fourteen lighting rods—fifteen if you have a ball retriever. No golfer wants to become a Christmas tree even though he or she knows the odds of surviving a lightning strike are nine out of ten. Golfers do have, after all, a lick of sense, as my grandpa used to say.

Golfers do love stories, and every golfer has at least one. The essence of a good story is that it is told in the first person, so let me tell one of mine.

This was not my regular foursome. Krebs is a big strong former Marine, the kind of guy seen on a recruiting poster, and he was kind of new to golf. Augie's a lawyer with more degrees than I can count, and some of the things he says I don't get until the next day. And then there's Tom, the ad man who once got paid for writing the now-famous words "Good stuff, Maynard" for a Malt-O-Meal commercial. I was the fourth, and I worked in manufacturing where I was learning all about plastics. It was Thursday. We had reached the eighth hole, and there were four skins riding on the outcome. We didn't gamble for much except our pride, and we had spent most of the round trying to get in the other guys' heads. It didn't matter who picked on whom; everyone was fair game. The eighth hole was a par four, not quite four hundred yards from the white tees. It was protected by a large pond with bunkers in front and to the left and right of the green. The fairway was lined by trees on the right and sloped to the pond, but flattened out a little the last thirty feet or so allowing for the ball to roll to a stop. It had a runout area to the left of the pond in the rough. The ideal tee shot would travel two hundred fifty yards, setting the golfer up for a second shot of one hundred forty yards to the front of the green.

On this particular day, everyone's drive was in good shape off the tee, and Krebs's ball had rolled right down to the water's edge. With his handicap, he laid there minus one and was twenty-five yards closer to the pin than anybody. We, of course, deemed it to be a lucky shot and began teasing him immediately about nearly going in the pond. All of us except Krebs hit our second shots, but no one was on the green. The door was wide open. In situations like this, the group's individual level of experience became a little unbalanced. Tom reminded Krebs that he needed to be very careful with his next shot as he was only a couple of feet from disaster, and we pulled the carts up pretty close to him to get a good look, but out of courtesy we got very quiet for his shot.

Krebs wanted the skins, loved the idea of kicking some butt on the real golfers, but more than anything he wanted the taste of victory. He got ready and swung, and his effort didn't disappoint us one bit. While trying to be so precise, he made a swing that he could have made in a phone booth, and he chunked the shot. It dropped into the water. We all smiled, but kept our giggles to ourselves. But who could resist a casual comment? Augie, being from Texas, went first, "Gust of wind took that ball right down." I added something he already knew, "I think that ball was short. You will have to drop another." Everyone was having fun except Krebs. Tom retrieved the divot, which was about the size of a monster cow pie, and then in a friendly gesture offered to clean Krebs's club. After a big sigh, Krebs dropped another ball, made a practice swing, and hit another ball. This ball was hit better than the first, but resulted in a second splash. For Krebs, this had now ceased to be fun. He dug into his bag for yet another ball, and Tom could not resist; he opened a beer and said, "I think we are going to be here for a while." Krebs not only got another ball, but he also changed clubs, studied the shot, teed it up, and then hit under the ball. This ball went straight up. Gulping his beer and looking up, Tom announced, "That could bring rain," just before another ball found a watery grave. I, for one, thought it was time to quit, but we all knew Krebs, and he never quits.

Augie, being Augie, suggested that Krebs go back to the drop area about twenty feet to his rear and regroup. So Krebs got into the golf cart, and we backed up to the drop area where he changed clubs again. No one made a sound. It is funny, but sometimes on the golf course it can get too quiet—almost as if some strange power waves its hand over the fairway and tells every living thing to shut up. This was one of those times. We could all feel it. Krebs lined up his shot, made his swing, and shanked the shot. This preordained ball whistled past Augie and barely missed Tom as if it were warning them to stay quiet. It then skipped four times across the pond reaching the other side and onto the bank where it remained motionless for several seconds. I could see a grin form on Krebs's face as he yelled, "Finally!" He had success at last, and I was happy for my friend. But then, for no explainable reason except possibly gravity, the ball lost its traction and began to roll backward ever so slowly at first and then gained momentum. We all watched as it dropped into the pond. At that point, I could tell that Krebs had finally lost it. What had happened was indeed harmful to his very soul—and this was a combat-tested Marine!

He walked back and forth. He appeared agitated, but in control, and he did not say a word. Several times he looked across the pond at the spot where his ball had been just minutes before. Still he said nothing. Finally, he looked at the drop area from where he had hit the ball, but he didn't drop another ball. He took a good stance and then a couple of practice swings and appeared to be lining up his shot without a ball. He then made what I would call a perfect swing, and he let his club fly. It sailed almost in slow motion out over Augie and Tom's golf cart.

The club was still airborne when the remark of the day came from the other cart. "Ahhh, that's going to be short too."

"That's it. I quit!" I heard him say to no one in particular. He got in the cart beside me, said nothing more, pushed the accelerator to the floor, and steered for the pond. I believe he had every intention of driving the cart right into the pond. I do not scare easily, but this scared me. Now, it would have been fun to see Krebs sink that cart, but I had no desire to take that ride with him to the bottom, and my clubs were on the back. I shouted, "Stop—not with me!" and some other words that Marines often share in moments of stress. He looked at me and brought the cart to a halt just short of the pond. He dismounted, unstrapped and shouldered his clubs, and headed for the bridge, crossing over the drainage creek from the pond. I turned to Augie and Tom and inquired, "You know it was funny, but who made that final insult?" Each of them pointed at the other guy. I shook my head and followed Krebs. I yelled at him, trying to get him to stop and rejoin us, but he didn't hear a thing I said. At midbridge, he came to a halt and hurled his bag into the pond with clubs flying everywhere. Without looking back, he cut off the cart path and headed down the creek line to the clubhouse.

The end of this story is simple. We had to let other golfers play through while we waded up to our necks into the pond to retrieve the bag and the clubs, and, worse yet, it took about an hour to locate the nine iron because we weren't paying attention when he threw it and hadn't seen where it landed. There are three lessons in this story. First, golf is just a game, so we've got to keep all emotions under control. Second, when friends are having a bad patch, it's not funny. We need to be supportive because the next bad patch might be our own. Third, always watch where the nine iron goes. The postscript to the above story is that we found Krebs sitting on the patio at the clubhouse where he was working on a cooler of ice-cold beer, and, true to his nature, he made an apology, and there were several other apologies to follow. I was just happy no one was hurt. We were wet; Krebs was dry and very happy to get his clubs back. We drank beer, we told stories, we drank more beer, we dried out, we laughed, we drank more beer, they closed the club, we all shook hands. Golf is great.

The atmosphere upon entering almost any clubhouse on a weekend around noon or a little after as the morning rounds are ending would be familiar to any golfer, and it wouldn't matter whether it was a room paneled in high-dollar burl wood, with sixty-six-degree air conditioning quietly circulating light cigar smoke away from the mahogany tables or a room with windows and doors wide open and furnished only with card tables closely spaced on a linoleum floor where the three ceiling fans are working overtime fighting to circulate the eighty-eight-degree air because the swamp cooler is busted.

In either case, golfers would recognize that, although the dress code may be worlds apart, the cast of characters is essentially the same. They're golfers, and they are huddled around the tables, scorecards displayed with numbers, circles, boxes, lines, and dollar signs with one official soul at each table now in control of the outcome of the morning's efforts. He or she will decide who's up and who's down, and those decisions will not be challenged. It is not so much the veracity of the totals or which decisions are made, it is the fact, pure and simple, that no one but a fellow golfer would want this job.

The wagers could be large or small or, in some cases, nonexistent, but they are of no real consequence because the golfers don't come for the money; they come for the play of game, the competition, and to do something with friends that has a beginning and end with an established order. I will not minimize the importance of winning for that is the purpose of keeping score, but sometimes winning among your friends is not as important as winning against yourself and against that constant competitor called Old Man Par that Bobby Jones wrote about so frequently.

Par was established and given significance for the ages by the Ladies' Golf Union of Great Britain under the direction of Miss Issette Pearson in 1896. The women were better organized than the men, and their system of par prevailed and became the standard method on golf courses throughout Great Britain. When news of this system reached the United States, the Massachusetts Golf Association tried to resist the use of the par system within the United States and wanted to maintain the more commonly used and easier bogey system. They failed.

I believe that there were some very strong and foresighted female golfing deities who could see the wisdom of Miss Pearson's thinking. Par refers to a standard score that golfers are trying to meet or beat, whether for a single hole or a collection of holes. If the first hole is a par four, for example, that means that the best golfers are expected to need four strokes to play it. Because of that, four is the score that all golfers want to meet (or beat), which is a very high standard indeed. So, in effect, when golfers play against par, they are playing against the projected score that the very best golfers would get on each hole every time they tee it up. Old Man Par, therefore, is quite a worthy opponent.

One lesson I learned from reading the books written by the Legends is that golfers never stop learning in this game. Golf is a game with many unanswered questions, and it starts in the pro shop, which can be an intimidating place. On anyone's first trip into a golf pro shop, he or she will find many new terms and lots of new equipment. Some shops have a library-like quietness to them, while others will be like any sporting-goods store—except for the prices. In contrast, the city park pro shops have displays that are more user friendly and, for the most part, so are the prices. Throughout the years, I have learned that there are no questions that shouldn't be asked. I have also learned that there are many answers given that are not worth hearing, so we shouldn't take every answer we hear as gospel. If someone advises us to stray too far from the tried-and-true fundamentals of the Legends, we need to be skeptical.

Golf is an experience sport, and we have to play the game over and over again to understand what our real questions are and to put any answers we receive into practice. The interesting thing about our game is that not all questions that come to mind while playing golf have to do with technique or fundamentals or are necessarily about golf itself. These questions could be about controlling emotions, about strategy, behavior, or fairness, and the most memorable lessons almost always happen when we least expect them.

There is not a golfer alive who wouldn't stand in line to get a lesson, or just a few words of wisdom, from Jack Nicklaus. Those words would be etched in your mind forever. It would be a dream come true. The golfer who illustrated this book happens to be my lifelong friend, and he has had just such an opportunity. It was an impromptu lesson, but I believe well worth sharing. What follows is Tom's recollection of the event.

"The year was 1980. My advertising agency, Martin-Williams, was shooting its annual advertising videos for E-Z-GO golf carts. The E-Z-GO cart was used at all the Nicklaus courses, and having Jack do one of the promotions was a natural. As creative director, I was the one chosen to go to Muirfield in Ohio to oversee the shoot. I was really psyched about the opportunity. This was a key promotion for E-Z-GO, and, as an avid golfer, just being at Muirfield would be a real plus, not to mention that I would be directing the one-and-only Jack Nicklaus. This was a dream assignment.

"I met Jack on the first tee, and I tried to be as professional as possible even though I was feeling quite intimidated on the inside. I then turned to the business at hand with my crew, which settled me. While I made certain that everything was set for the shoot, Jack took a seat on a nearby bench, watching intently as I finalized preparations.

"As I began to talk, I noticed Jack's MacGregor bag standing upright on the tee just a few feet away from me. While and I was explaining how the shoot would take place, I casually pulled Jack's driver from his bag. I was in the zone. I had the rapt attention of the best golfer in the world, and I was telling him what was going to happen and what he was going to do. I felt bulletproof. The words rolled off my tongue in a perfect cadence explaining his role. I had my feet spread shoulder width apart, my arms were extended in front of me with my hands balanced on Jack's club.

I was thinking that surely I must look and sound really in charge of this shoot. I explained how he would say a few well-chosen words about how great E-Z-GO carts are and then he was to take his driver and smash a ball down the fairway.

"God, I thought I was doing great! I was giving instructions to one of the true legends of golf, and he was really focused in on every word. I was about to make another good point when Jack rose slowly to his feet, and he kind of cocked his head to the right like he does before he really smashes a long drive. The temperature on the tee box dropped about twenty degrees, and I would swear to this day that as far as I was concerned everything stopped. The birds stopped chirping, the clouds ceased to move, my battery-powered Timex quit, and I, of course, stopped speaking midsentence. It was absolutely quiet when Jack asked, in a voice that sounded like my mother inquiring about poop in my pants when I was old enough to know better, 'Is that my driver?' I wanted so much to answer 'no,' but I had to say 'yes.'

"He looked at me for just a few seconds as if he were measuring me, trying to comprehend whether or not I would be able to understand the lesson he was about to give me. He then exhaled and said, 'That club has a leather grip, and you're holding it upside down with the grip in the grass. The grass is wet, and that could wreck the leather. Never do that to a club.' I immediately shrunk to so small a size that I felt I was barely visible peeking out over my size-eleven Johnson Murphys and tried to mumble an apology."

Thirty-six years have passed since that day, and Tom's recollection of the event is still vivid. Like all favorite golf stories, it also gets better with the telling. We all know that the basic truth remains: don't put leather grips in wet grass, and, perhaps the bigger truth, if the chance to impress the Big Dog comes, it is not the time to be standing there with an open fly and a runny nose.

Our game is more than seven hundred years old, and it would take more than just a few pages to explain all there is to know about a game that has become a weekly ritual in the lives of so many generations. The National Golf Foundation publishes statistics putting the number of players in the United States at around twenty-five million. There are twelve thousand courses in the United States that are members of the Golf Handicap Information Network (GHIN)—a system that is designed to promote equitable play among players of unequal ability. Unfortunately, fewer than 10 percent of all golfers are serious enough about the game to have a registered handicap.

There are truly some players of the game who love to hit balls and don't really care about their scores. Some of them play reasonably good golf, too. They are the ones that have learned to play the game shot by shot—each shot bringing a new challenge and potential for success. When each shot is over, it's over. Such a golfer was my older brother. He loved the game. When they retired, he and his wife built a great house on the tenth fairway of a beautiful golf course called Kahite in Tellico Village, Tennessee. He even started his own golf group—a Wednesday morning group who believed that the breakfast and camaraderie were as much a part of the day as the golf. He often would call me to talk, and there would always be The Shot—not always his shot, but The Shot, and we would discuss it in some detail. He was a truly great guy, a loving husband, a highly decorated Marine, a friend to anyone who needed one, and a golfer. He died unexpectedly from an accidental fall at his home. We held a memorial service befitting a golfer; it was held on the tenth tee of the Kahite Golf Course. Dick would have been embarrassed by the size of the crowd, but would have loved greeting so many friends and neighbors. After the service when things had settled down, I took his urn, and the two of us had one last ride around the course because I needed one last round with my big brother. That trip around the course gave me a chance for a private goodbye.

Reading the volumes of instructional information offered on our subject can be rewarding, but it can also be confusing. All golfers should be cautioned against changing instruction paths or instructors too frequently. I have read and reread the books written by the men I've chosen as the seven Legends to be the backbone of this book. Each of them was convinced of the same thing. The fundamentals are the basis of a sound golf game, and perfect practice is the key to learning the fundamentals. Fortunately for me in my studies, I did not have to bounce around between ideas because they wrote the same information over and over. The process was like watching my favorite movies over and over again. There always seemed to be something that I missed the time before that would make the rereading worthwhile. In my mind, the advice these men have to offer is not to be taken lightly. Their achievements speak for themselves, and their thoughts about how to play our game are not only accurate, but also reinforced by each other and by my own decades of experience.

What I did find was a slight tone of apology that drifts subconsciously through some of their writing that seems to say, "We are sorry that the way golf instruction has been handled makes our game seem so difficult to learn." I think this has happened because there is so much about golf that is unteachable through the written word, and these men knew it. The game of golf is an experience sport. That experience will be gained both explicitly and implicitly, and it will take time.

So, we have a sport that is difficult to learn and one that is sometimes taught by professionals who make it more difficult because they think they can explain it all when they can't. I am always wary of those who talk too much. Simple is best. Often the very best advice comes to us in the strangest places—like the tenth row in a movie theater while watching the movie *The Legend of Bagger Vance*. Old Bagger sums up Junuh's problem with golf by describing it as "a game that can't be won, it can only be played."[10] Now that is a message only those who have played a lot of golf can understand, and those golfers who understand the message have already accomplished much.

Aristotle said, "The one exclusive sign of thorough knowledge is the power of teaching." I believe that if I can teach just one golf skill to someone else, it is a sign that I fully understand what I have learned, and understanding is the essence of learning. Every time I observe someone hit a ball there is a lesson in that action for me, and I should take the time to learn from it. The same is true for every golfer out there; there is a lesson in every round, so learn from it.

The gods of failure can invade the game and destroy our confidence. They can make it difficult to draw our clubs back. They will try to do this. It's then that the game ceases to be fun. It is then that you need a reality check or a safety valve. Arnold Palmer offers up some no-nonsense advice for those moments that feel like the train has left the station with our luggage in it, leaving us still standing on the platform. "The next time you go out on the golf course, forget the fancy theory, shake your inferiority complex, give the ball a good healthy whack—and enjoy yourself."[11] What Arnie is saying is to stop thinking so much; no one can think himself around the golf course. If we start trying to control our swings on the course by thinking while we are swinging, we are in trouble. Thinking about it in that moment will only get us in the way of our swing.

Golf can hold its head high in the sports hierarchy. When the greatest athletic champions of all times are ranked, it is interesting to note that golf champions are ranked right up along with the noted basketball, football, and soccer legends. On a list compiled by a noted Australian writing group in 2009 comparing the top one hundred all-time athletes, there were six golfers on the all-time list, and three of those were in the top twenty. To me, that says a lot about what it takes to be a champion golfer.

2
The Legends

Once the round is underway, the business at hand becomes that of getting results. Nothing else matters.
—Bobby Jones

In the introduction, I wrote about trust being the foundation of self-confidence. I explained that trust in one's golf game develops when it is built upon sound fundamentals as taught by the seven Legends. These are men who have earned the right to be called Legends through their accomplishments on and off the golf course. They played and lived the game of golf, earning the respect of their peers and golf fans throughout the world. These Legends have written about what they learned in order to pass this knowledge on to the next generations of golfers. It is well worth taking time to highlight these men—what they have said and something about their lives.

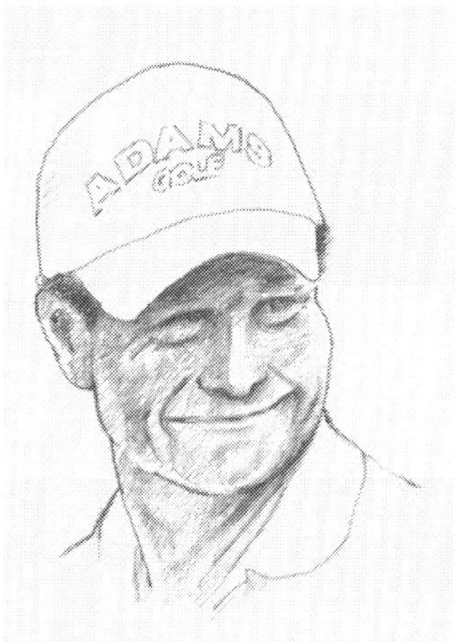

Our first story involves Tom Watson on a day that was really all about golf magic. I would say that the tension was tight, even tighter than a bridge cable, when fifty-nine-year-old Tom Watson walked to the last tee of the Open Championship at Turnberry in 2009. He needed to make one final par to win. How completely improbable the possibility of his victory seemed three days earlier! London bookmakers had the five-time British Open winner at long odds even to make the cut. The rain and wind were too much for some—Tiger Woods, who was ranked number one in the world, retired early, missing the cut along with David Duval, Sandy Lyle, Nick Faldo, and Greg Norman. But on this day, fate and the golfing gods brought Watson through to the eighteenth and final tee with victory at hand. The crowd at Ayrshire, Scotland, the home of the Turnberry course, and those crouched in front of televisions around the world simply had no frame of reference against which to measure

Figure 2.1 Tom Watson

the feat they witnessed that day. Having gone four-three-four, he was cumulatively one under for the first three rounds on the eighteenth, having dominated this hole for three consecutive days. Television commentators nearly ran out of superlatives to describe what they were watching, and they felt sure they were about to anoint a champion. But as it is with many stories, it was too good to be true. The gods of golf do not grant miracles easily, and certainly the gods were involved as they set up one more test for Watson. He had survived the day by playing with guts and heart, and the fifty-nine year old steadied his nerves one more time to hit his second shot—an eight iron. In flight it looked perfect, but the ball took a bad hop on the green and ended up bounding past the hole and stopping just inches into the first cut. Tom chose to putt and left himself an eight footer coming back. Watson steadied himself for one last effort. It was now all or nothing. The putt was not one of Watson's best and rolled up short and to the right of the hole and with it went Watson's hopes for the Open Championship. It would probably be true to say that anyone watching knew that for every inch that ball rolled it was drawing the final strength from what was left of Watson's reserve. Any real chance he had to clinch this historic victory depended on that ball finding the bottom of the cup. Tom Watson lost to Stewart Cink in a four-hole playoff by six strokes.

Now, why have I chosen to feature a loss like this when Watson had plenty of victories about which I could have written? I do not consider it a loss. At age fifty-nine, Tom Watson produced more winning golf in those four days than most golfers will produce in a lifetime.

In many ways, this loss is equal to the win that a forty-six-year-old Jack Nicklaus produced at the 1986 Masters, which might be considered his most exciting win of all time. Like in Watson's case, the bookies didn't give him a chance. Augusta National takes a toll on everyone who plays, and the Masters is a tournament that very few have dominated. There are always a few opening rounds that come in low and get everyone excited, but the final day punishes everyone. The 1986 tournament looked to be a battle between Greg Norman, Tom Kite, and Seve Ballesteros. Jack was trailing throughout the front nine, and, at age forty-six, he was no longer referred to as the

Figure 2.2 Jack Nicklaus

Golden Bear. He was past his prime, and those who followed him around the course were more students of the game who acknowledged his legendary status than hopeful fans sensing victory. His Saturday round showed some signs that the fires were still burning, and he began on Sunday under par but off the pace. At the eleventh hole Jack was in the fight, but then a bogey seemed to take him out, and the crowd turned toward Kite and Norman. Then something happened. Jack birdied thirteen and went on to play the last six holes in five under finishing with an eighteen-hole total of 279. And then he waited. Kite missed a twelve footer for birdie to tie, and Norman sailed it wide to the right on his second shot and couldn't get up and down. Nicklaus won his sixth green jacket.

Both these outings of Jack and Watson are examples of men well past their golfing prime demonstrating golfing brilliance; one did it in victory and one in defeat. These men have earned the admiration of the entire golfing world through their sportsmanship, dedication to the sport, and respect of the game. I believe Watson's loss will go down as the greatest effort in a loss in the history of golf. Nicklaus, on the other hand, is already known as the greatest golfer of all time with eighteen career victories in major tournaments. However, those victories alone do not define his career. Jack knows what it is like to taste defeat. He has nineteen runner-up finishes in major tournaments, which is more than any other golfer in history, and he placed third in nine. One can only wonder how many times one little bounce of that white ball changed history and the outcome for Jack, Watson, and the other Legends.

There is plenty written about how stoic Nicklaus is, but little is written about his humorous side. I am not trying to paint Jack as a comedian because he is not, but the 1971 US Open playoff video with Lee Trevino showed that Jack has a less serious side. Trevino and Nicklaus were tied after seventy-two holes in the 1971 US Open, and Trevino was in the mood for some mischief before another day of golf began. He arrived at the first tee, where tensions are usually very high, and Trevino disappointed no one. He produced a snake. This was not a small snake, and in the video this snake looked real, but it was from a photo shoot Trevino had just completed. Jack was sitting across the tee box from Trevino when the snake was pulled out. Seeing the snake doesn't upset Jack or even faze him; in fact, he went right along with the spoof and asked Lee if he could see the snake. Trevino heaved the snake across the tee box, and the crowd erupted in laughter. The tension was broken. What a memorable start to the US Open playoff!

Jack later commented that every day was April Fool's Day for Lee. It was a great match, even though Jack lost the playoff by three strokes, but not because of the appearance of the snake. It was Trevino's year, and he went on to win both the Canadian Open and the British Open.

All of us will experience, or have already experienced, the disaster of having a tremendous shot ruined by a bad bounce or will watch, or have already watched, as a crucial putt veers off line, moved by an unseen break or pebble on the green. Like any golfer, Jack Nicklaus has had his share of bad results from good shots and warns us all, "Keep your cool—accept the fact that golf was never meant to be a 100 percent fair game, and that you are human and therefore fallible."[12]

Jack is a winner and a realist, and his record of achievement is validation of just that philosophy. Jack has taken the good bounces along with the bad and knows that things can go wrong on and off the course. To succeed, everyone must learn that lesson. It is difficult to see one of the very best shots ruined by a bad bounce, but it happens every day in golf just as it happens in life.

Golf is a hard game to figure out. Perhaps we never will. One would think it would get easier the more someone plays it, but Bobby Jones explains that golf doesn't work that way, "Golf is the only game I know of that actually becomes harder the longer you play it."[13] Puzzling? Jones is talking from the perspective of someone who is seeking perfection in a game where perfection can never be reached. Improvements can always be made up to a certain level, and then, even for the truly excellent players, fine-tuning happens every time the hand grips a club. Every golfer will reach a certain point when maintenance begins and staying at the same level of competence is a constant battle because it means practicing things over and over again that have already been learned.

Arnold Palmer wrote my favorite description of golf using very few words, "Golf is deceptively simple and endlessly complicated."[14] In my opinion, that is the most accurate description of our game ever written. For anyone who doesn't yet play and doesn't understand or for those who play and still need clarification, try substituting the word *sex* for golf, and that should illustrate the idea Palmer was trying to get across about the fundamentals and the boundaries of golf being both simple and complex at the same time.

In Palmer's book, *My Game and Yours*, he describes playing golf in the early spring as a youth in Latrobe, Pennsylvania, and gives the reader a special insight into his view of the world of golf. He would sometimes find himself physically on the course, but really being spiritually or mentally somewhere else and having to work hard to "get down to business."[15] He explains that there are times when golf is not at all about playing the game; it's about enjoying the setting, getting away from work, clogged freeways, congested streets, overbuilt neighborhoods, and finding peace and happiness on the fairways and greens of our favorite pastime. The golf course can represent a place of freedom, solitude, and relief from other worldly matters. It could be the smell of the grass, hot dogs at the turn, the flight of that little ball, or just the camaraderie of our buddies. Sometimes nothing can compare with the simple time spent on the course. Those who play the game regularly know, like Arnie, that when we're playing golf, we are temporarily otherwise absorbed.

Arnie is one of very few individuals to have his own favorite drink made up by and shared first with a bartender, then with his local golfing community, then the golfing world, and now the Arnold Palmer is universally enjoyed. It is a mixture of 50 percent tea and 50 percent lemonade.

As the story goes, Arnie stepped up to the bar in Palm Springs and explained to the bartender that he wanted a specific mixture of tea and lemonade. A lady overheard his request and told the bartender that she too would like one of those "Palmer drinks." The lemonade-iced tea drink is now famous. Anybody for an Arnold Palmer?

Golf is one of the few professional sports in the world that remains self-regulated even at the highest levels of competition. Every golfer has a responsibility to play the game by the rules since there are no umpires or officials running alongside the players calling fouls and issuing penalties. This self-regulation is unusual in an age when, in other professional sports, even the most famous players and teams break rules to achieve the

Figure 2.3 Arnold Palmer

slightest advantage and try to get away with it. There seems to be a public outcry about such behavior only when and if they get caught, not because the cheating happens in the first place.

Recently, in the world of professional football, Deflategate clearly illustrates this point. One of the most famous quarterbacks in all professional football, his team's management, and even fans denied what appeared to be obvious to anyone reading the facts. The team was playing with underinflated balls. They knew they were breaking a rule. Perhaps it is not a big rule, but it's a rule. The outcry from the fans came not because they learned that their team was breaking a rule, but because the rule was enforced. Whenever people become upset when rules are enforced, we could invoke the Sam Snead statement, "Something's wrong somewhere."

How rules are enforced in the game of golf, with professionals self-regulating, seems to make a big difference. We cannot imagine a player at the US Open saying noodling the ball isn't really breaking the rules, when we all know it is, nor can we imagine fans supporting a player who made such claims. Deflategate happened and yet legendary golfers call penalties on themselves with championship titles at stake.

One good example of this actually happening involves Bobby Jones. He received considerable notoriety and praise in 1925 at the US Open at the Worcester Country Club. Jones called a penalty on himself for a ball that moved. The ball was in a position where only Jones could see it move, but he insisted that it had, and the penalty stroke cost him the US Open. When news of the event was printed, Jones was quoted as saying, "You might as well praise a man for not robbing a bank as praise him for playing by the rules."[16] Was the movement of that ball important? It was insignificant to the play of the hole, but it was important to Jones to keep his personal integrity intact, and that is the difference between being legendary and being notorious. Keeping personal integrity as a top priority

Figure 2.4 Bobby Jones

creates a fine example for participants and fans of golf. Ask the NFL fans what is important, and they might just give a different answer.

Jones has shared his knowledge of golf by writing more than five hundred thousand words printed in news and sports articles; not only that, he demonstrated the game in eighteen movie shorts and wrote five books on the subject. His feelings about the game are expressed as follows, "Golf in my view, is the most rewarding of all games because it possesses a very definite value as a 'moulder' or developer of character. The golfer very soon is made to realize that his most immediate, and perhaps his most potent, adversary is himself."[17]

His most lasting influence has been his creation of the Augusta National Golf Club and the Masters Tournament. Players at the first-ever Masters Tournament in 1935 attended by his invitation only. The Masters is now one of the four majors, and it is played in the first full week of April. Unlike the other majors, it has a permanent venue and is always played in Augusta, Georgia. To

Figure 2.5 Harvey Penick

see the place is to understand why. There is absolutely no better place in the world for a golf tournament. My grandmother's living room was not as immaculate as this golf course, and no detail, even down to monitoring the lines at the bathrooms, is overlooked.

Upon arriving, library manners kick into full gear even when walking the grounds. Bushels of politeness and hospitality are available from the ever-abundant members of the Masters Tournament staff who almost seem to be talking in hushed tones as they effectively manage the crowds. I will not attempt to describe the course. Most golfers have all seen it on television many times, and for a golfer to be there on the grounds and see it in person is a little like a first visit to the US Capitol, the White House, or all the monuments. It is really that special.

Besides the Masters, there are three other major professional championships played each year: the PGA, the US Open, and the British Open. Winning all four of these in a calendar year is called the modern grand slam of golf. No one has ever accomplished that feat. In 1930, Bobby Jones won the US and British amateurs and both professional opens, which was considered at the time to be the grand slam. He retired at the age of twenty-eight in poor health, and his feat has never been duplicated. Since that time, only five golfers have won what is called the career grand slam; those golfers are Gene Sarazen, Ben Hogan, Gary Player, Jack Nicklaus, and Tiger Woods.

There have been many high-profile incidents during which golfers have given up much because keeping personal integrity intact was more important than winning. Harvey Penick wrote about one time when Tom Kite advised his fellow competitor that he might get a penalty if he continued his current course of action. The opponent reversed his play and won the tournament by one stroke over Tom Kite. It wasn't just any old tournament; it was the US Open, and the incident happened during the final round. Penick remarked, "An Open Champion is a winner on the golf course. A person of honor is a winner everywhere."[18] Kite could have kept his mouth shut and won the US Open, but that is not the way our game is played.

The game is a constant challenge, and the opportunity for success is reborn on every hole; in fact, the opportunity is reborn on every shot because that is how the game is played—one shot at a time. A golfer can accumulate victories hole by hole or shot by shot; he or she gets to choose. I have mentioned the gods of golf several times, and, although I have no empirical proof of their existence at this stage in my life, I am certain they exist. There is no explaining what happens in our game by any other means. They are around to deal out good and bad fortune in equal measure no matter the stature of the player. It is important to know that whatever they deal out should be considered tests and not penalties. They only give us what we can handle. They haunt every clubhouse, walk hand in hand down every fairway, and surround every green. There is not a golfer alive who has any way of knowing which one he or she is going to meet, but there are some golfers who have a sense about these gods and their presence.

The gods of failure often wear the disguise of success, hoping to lure us into trying a shot we have no business attempting. In my first book, *Golf from the Ground Up*, I described this god as an entity called Stupid. I went on to tell a story about when Jean Van de Velde was on the eighteenth hole in 1999 at Carnoustie. His eventual loss was a result of his giving in to this character called Stupid right there on the eighteenth hole. It was easy to explain and easy to understand. Stupid was also responsible for Phil Mickelson's poor decisions on the eighteenth hole at Winged Foot when he had his US Open title in hand. Now, Stupid could be a tag name for the entire genre of golfing gods who are still hard at work causing golfers to make poor decisions that cost them strokes on every round every day. I say genre because I cannot imagine how only one such deity could cover so much ground and produce so much havoc on such a regular basis.

The most notable attack lately was at the 2016 Masters when someone usually so totally in command of himself and his game on the golf course let Stupid inside his head—not once, but twice, and it cost him the Masters. Jordan Spieth came to the twelfth after playing some shaky golf, but still in command of the tournament. He set up to play the hole where his shot would have been a draw, his favored shot, and somewhere in the process he changed his mind and hit a fade—and a weak fade at that. The ball ended up in the water. Moving to shot number two, now lying three, Spieth once again listened to Stupid. Instead of going to the drop zone where he would be 100 percent sure of the distance, he hit from the fairway eighty odd yards from the hole. He was making a judgment call on the distance, and Jordan admitted this later. For the second time in two swings, he added additional doubt to his already shaky game and hit a fat shot barely getting it to the water—kerplunk! Now Spieth had to hit his fifth shot on a par three, and he was not yet on the green. He two putted for a quadruple bogey. His Masters lead was gone, and so was any chance he had of winning.

Yes, it's true; I believe in the gods of golf. They test us and sometimes we fail. We just don't expect failure from our heroes. Stupid has been around challenging golfers since they invented scorecards. The suggestion I make to all golfers in my first book is to conduct a thorough exorcism on our golf bags at the beginning of each new season and before big matches to assure ourselves that we have removed Stupid. We should always remember that he will try to influence our choice of shots whenever he can through compliments about how strong our golf game is in spite of physical evidence to the contrary. He will turn a small mistake into a big one every time.

Harvey Penick, golf instructor, philosopher, and a guy anyone would like to have for a friend, would talk about bad patches on the course and reminds us, "…golf and life are similar. There's nothing guaranteed to be fair in either golf or life and we shouldn't expect it to be different. You must accept your disappointments and triumphs equally."[19] That is Harvey at his best, digging deep and coming up with some real old philosophy. I know what he means because I found something similar handed down from a guy born twenty-five hundred years ago in Lumbini, in what is now Nepal. I'm pretty sure they didn't play golf back then, but his advice has been invaluable to a great number of people throughout the ages: "Do not dwell in the past, do not dream of the future, concentrate the mind on the present moment." Now that's good advice for any golfer, and it's from the prince Shakyamuni Buddha.

Buddha would have probably made an excellent golf instructor or commentator, and I think he would have been a good friend of Harvey's. He would understand that no one can play our game worried about what just happened with the shot he just hit because it's already history. Nor can anyone play the game thinking about what might happen in the future because it is unpredictable. What we each must do is to play our best golf and concentrate our efforts on what we can control, which is the shot about to be played—nothing more and nothing less.

Figure 2.6 Ben Hogan

It is necessary to adopt a mind-set that in the game of golf the goal of perfection is not ever going to be attained. Bobby Jones wrote, "One reason golf is such an exasperating game is that a thing learned is easily forgotten, and we find ourselves struggling year after year with faults we had discovered and corrected time and again."[20] So, as we find that we are having a problem with something we already know, we must remember that even the very best golfers have been in similar situations. Several of the Legends have commented on the number of perfect shots they might hit in each round of golf. They golf for a living, and yet, when confronted with the perfection question, the most they can come up with is maybe five shots per round. A golfer's objective should not be to hit perfect shots, but to reduce the amount each shot varies from the perfect shot. Anyone can reach a certain level of performance by simply playing the game, but real and lasting improvements will require practice. No golfer can play his or her way to a superior level of performance without practice, but it is also true that golfers cannot practice their way to a superior game.

The Legends of the game have spent their entire lives devoted to that end. They have honed their skills through days, weeks, and years of practice and play. They have learned to accept the fact that the game they play will not allow them to reach perfection, but it will allow them to hit perfect shots. For our Legends, this work has paid off in high-pressure championships earned at the highest levels of competition. This adherence to the fundamentals and devotion to practice has allowed them to achieve success even though mishits and bad bounces occur.

When Hogan describes what every golfer is looking for, he summarizes the quest as follows, "…that there is an explanation for everything that takes place, that the seeming mystery of how to hit the ball well and hit it well regularly is not mysterious at all, that it is possible to arrive at answers that will be clear-cut and irrefutable…."[21]

Hogan is saying that knowledge builds confidence. The more shots a golfer knows, the more confident he or she will be. All shots are based on fundamentals, and we cannot argue with Hogan's premise that the search goes on and on. In this book, we have a consensus of golf fundamentals using a group of golfing Legends, including Hogan, for direction. These golfers played the game as well as any who ventured out on the short grass and passed on the skills they acquired through years of instruction and dedicated practice. None of what they built their games on was learned overnight, and certainly they would not advertise that anyone could acquire the skills of golf over the weekend or from some gimmick or from some new golf gadget. I am confident that building a solid game depends on the ability to eliminate the margin of error in each shot that is made. Each shot is equally valuable, whether on the practice tee, the putting green, or on the golf course. From this day forward, there should be no throwaway shots.

Three of our Legends were at the 2014 Masters. Palmer and Nicklaus were honorary starters, and Watson was in the field, participating in his last Masters Tournament as a player. Observing the pros at work in the practice area was quite an education. I was amazed to realize that these men are generally smaller in real life than they appear on television. I turned to my friend, Tom, and, in hushed tones, said something like, "Gosh, I thought Watson was much bigger." Seeing these men on the same day was a lucky day, and I find it fitting that the Masters Champions are part of the tournament every year. Watching them hit and judging from the soundness of the ball strikes, I found myself thinking that there has to be some hidden secret that only the pros know that makes the magic we see on the television at all possible.

Maybe there are just one or two simple tricks of the trade, which the tour pros are keeping to themselves, that the golfing public doesn't know. If we could just watch them on the practice tee long enough and follow them around, we might learn that special secret. This has always been one of the great puzzlements of golf. Well, Watson gives us the truth of the matter: "Golf fans think the tour pros are on the practice range sharing secret insights to the swing and working on esoteric keys to which they, average golfers, are not privy.... Well I'm afraid we're not hiding anything.... We're out there working on tried and true fundamentals."[22] The words "tried and true fundamentals" should settle into our minds. Watson tells us that the skills he and the other pros are working on are not something special. They are not out on the practice tee talking about secret ways to hit the ball. They are fine-tuning their performance of the basic fundamentals. These are the same fundamentals that are available to all golfers, and they are right here in this book.

This should be takeaway lesson number one for every golfer reading this book. Poor performance or lack of knowledge about the fundamentals is the primary reason shots go astray. Looking for salvation in the latest magazine article or training gimmick or buying the newest club billed as a quick fix are all just a waste of time.

While watching a professional swing a golf club, it's easy to imagine owning a swing as smooth and consistent, but those swings are earned; they don't just happen. There is a significant commitment of time and effort involved in making those swings happen. The difference consists of hitting about fifty or one hundred balls only once a week or hitting at least fifty or one hundred balls every day. Sam Snead's swing has often been described as the most natural swing ever, and the one swing all golfers should try to emulate. Trying to estimate the number of balls he hit during his first forty years as a golfer, Sam discussed it with a friend, "We decided on 1,600,040."[23] That's right, one million six hundred thousand forty. That's how he developed a so-called natural swing. By the time he wrote *Golf Begins at Forty*, he was sixty-six years old and estimated that the number was "probably more than 2,000,000." And he went on to state that he "…never dreamed I'd still be playing some 250 rounds of golf per year at age sixty-five."[24] Only a true golfer with a love of the game would interrupt a hunting trip at age fifty-six to play a match in Nairobi against two of the best amateurs with borrowed clubs for a payoff of three leopard skins.

Figure 2.7 Sam Snead

Sam Snead was a man with an extraordinary love of the game. His advice to older golfers was "Play more. Enjoy more."[25] And if we do the math on those two million balls, it comes to about one hundred golf balls a day if we assume he started when he was ten years old. Playing golf is like being in a boat headed upstream—we must keep rowing. This is especially true when learning new skills or correcting faults. We must continue rowing every day or the current pulls the boat back downstream. Golfers need to consider what kind of commitment to the game of golf is necessary in order to achieve success. No one will have to hit one hundred balls every day for the next forty years before noticeable progress is made, but some kind of regular practice is a must. And in order to make sure practice time is not wasted, it is necessary that every aspect of the skills being practiced be based on solid fundamentals.

I believe those who say they play golf strictly for fun are just kidding themselves; we all want to swing the club just a little bit better each time we get the chance to swing again. Whether or not we tell anybody else what our goals are, every hole is a competition in the brain. We just can't help ourselves. That is the way we are all built; it's part of the human psyche. Whether we play against ourselves, Old Man Par, or a really friendly group of breakfast buddies, eventually, no matter what level of golf we choose to play, we are going to want to play better. Arnie recognized this when he wrote the phrase "get down to business" and said, "It is my earnest belief that a player must feel that he wants to play a very good game, else he will never play even a respectable game."[26] When we set out to learn, it's time to concentrate, and if we do concentrate, our efforts will pay off.

To close out these thoughts on golf, let me finish by saying, again, that golf is so much like life that no matter who tries to explain its meaning we won't understand it until we experience it on our own. Golf is a game where the smallest thing can mark our very biggest days. It is a game where lessons don't always come from mistakes, and not every lesson is something that can be recorded on the scorecard. It is a game that begins with a club and some balls and ends up being a journey into oneself. What we all learn from our game is that making mistakes is proof that we are trying, so we must stop being afraid of what could go wrong and think of what could go right and, as the Legends would advise, play the game with passion. We are only restricted by the barriers we create for ourselves.

There are some things we can always get back, but time isn't one of them. Every day spent waiting for our games to improve without doing something about it is an opportunity lost forever. To paraphrase Einstein, "If we keep doing what we are doing, we're going to keep getting what we're getting." Success is hard work. If we want to build a golf game, we have work to do. One of the all-time great motivators in all of sports was the Green Bay Packers' coach Vince Lombardi, and he said, "The man on top of the mountain didn't fall there."

Part II

3
Learning to Learn

Learning how to learn is life's most important skill.
—Tony Buzan

In part I, I wrote about seven individuals whose teaching could make anyone into a better golfer. That is not a certainty, but it is a possible outcome. All it takes to make success more probable is to understand what those golf Legends are offering and to practice the fundamentals in an orderly manner until they are mastered. The extra ingredient offered in this chapter is information about how to process the material and put it into action so that the ideas and theories and strategies gleaned from the Legends will yield better golf games.

Before I am accused of wandering too far from the fundamentals of golf, let me set the stage. In 2009 I wrote a book, *Golf from the Ground Up*. The chapter titled "The Brain Is Boss" explained that the golfer trains his or her brain, not the muscles, and that learning happened in three phases, each requiring considerable practice—especially for golfers over the age of twenty. That was a good, but insufficient, explanation.

The subject of learning is a very broad field, and we are dealing with just a corner of that field. We are dealing with behavior modification. In every learned behavior, the first thing that happens is discovery. In order to learn to play the game of golf, the first thing that had to happen was that someone had to discover each action or fundamental that was necessary to play the game. These fundamentals were learned, then taught to others, and finally shared through the generations from that day until now. As the game became more sophisticated, there have been modifications to those fundamentals, and the teachings were updated to reflect changes in play or teaching methods, creating a continuum of discovery, change, and teaching followed by another cycle of discovery, change, and teaching and so on. Evaluations of today's fundamentals show that there have been very few changes during the past forty years. There have been minor modifications to how instructors teach the fundamentals, but, essentially, we are teaching the same golf fundamentals that were being taught forty years ago.

Most people who start to play the game of golf today venture out to play without formal instruction. They learn to play by discovery, or self-teaching. Golf can be learned this way, but not very efficiently. We do know of professional golfers who have been self-taught, so we must draw the conclusion that learning by the discovery or self-teaching method can work, but that method generally works best when a golfer starts at a young age. Starting after the age of twenty slows the learning process considerably, progress is frequently stalled, and skills are often left incomplete because the learner does not fully understand the learning process. Having improper learning skills is at the root of improvement plateaus, not any lack of either physical or mental ability.

Everyone who watches golf being played, either on television or in person, has gone through at least some part of the learning process because the brain, without conscious effort, has the ability to store information about every aspect of golf. As we see others swing golf clubs or walk up to a tee box and place a ball, our brains are tucking this information away for future reference. This is learning discovery and called implicit learning; we have only observed and have done nothing physically. This kind of information may not be very helpful when the time comes for actually playing the game, but, nevertheless, the brain is learning. If someone begins to swing a golf club and begins to hit golf balls, however, the brain starts receiving feedback from all five senses, and this information also gets stored as discovery information about the game of golf. Beginning to take golf lessons or reading an instruction manual about the game would be called explicit learning.

What needs to be understood about motor-skill learning is that the muscles have not been taught to do anything. There is no such thing as muscle memory. The muscles receive all their instructions, good or bad, through stimuli from the brain. The brain gathers and stores information received by the five senses, and it is responsible for building the skills and habits a golfer brings to the course when he plays golf. This chapter focuses on how the brain learns from outside information and what we can do to assist the brain in its effort to make us each the best golfer possible given our individual capabilities.

I am not a neurologist, nor will I pretend to be, and this chapter is not an attempt to be a lesson in neurology. It is because of my interest in posttraumatic stress and traumatic brain injury that I have spent a great deal of time learning about the science of the brain for the past ten years. Part of the work I have done is to help veterans realize that the brain is plastic, which means it can adapt to varying conditions, and its patterns are not permanent. Whatever the brain has learned can be changed—unlearned or relearned. During the 1960s and 1970s, the primary brain scanning technologies of positron emission tomography (PET) scan, functional magnetic resonance imaging (MRI), and magneto-encephalography (MEG) were developed. The machines used for these tests are beyond my understanding, but their invention and continued advancements have allowed scientists to effectively scan the brain to observe cognitive activities, or what we call thinking, by taking pictures of the brain while it is in action making muscles contract and relax. This ability to observe the brain in action has completely changed brain science. Neurologists no longer have to guess how things happen; this technology allows for the study of the brain to more precisely illuminate the learning process.

Dr. Mortimer J. Adler explains, "A human habit isn't formed by having something done to you; a human habit is formed by your doing something."[27] Having something done to a person is a passive behavior like reading about how to grip the golf club or having an instructor tell someone about how to form the grip and then placing that student's hands on the club in the correct position. Afterward, the student may think he has the grip position in his mind, but he has never actually constructed it physically. Even after the student has seen it done and has had his hands placed on the club correctly, he still has to physically do it, which is another problem entirely. It will not matter how many times this is done for the student or how often he reads about the correct way to do it, he will never learn the proper grip until he participates in forming the grip himself and practices putting his own hands in the proper grip on the club by himself. This repetitive practice is the key action in acquiring all motor skills.

By watching thoughts make changes in the brain, neurologists can tell when learning occurs, and this doesn't happen unless the student is actively involved in the process. The more brain activity there is, the more changes are observed and more genuine learning takes place. We have all been told at one time or another to put on our thinking caps. As it turns out, neurologically speaking, that was not bad advice. The brain is covered with a cap of neurons that is approximately one inch thick. This layer of cells is called the cerebrum or big brain. This is where the action takes place.

In the frontal lobe of the cerebrum is the frontal cortex. This is the cognitive, or thinking, brain where the three stages of the learning process begin. The first stage, the cognitive stage, takes place in the frontal cortex. When we try a new motor skill, it is in the frontal cortex where conscious brain activity takes place. As soon as a person thinks about what he wants to do, in the form of either a conscious or an unconscious thought, the frontal cortex sorts out all the motor processes necessary to complete the action. Neurotransmitters, which are chemicals, are activated, and, through a process of synaptic connection, electrical signals are sent via neurons from the cerebral cortex to the motor cortex in the midbrain to the cerebellum in the lower brain and back to the motor cortex and then down the spine to the necessary muscles, and the action is completed.

The first time a person attempts a motor skill, the skill is performed by a series of independent actions, and nothing is held in a

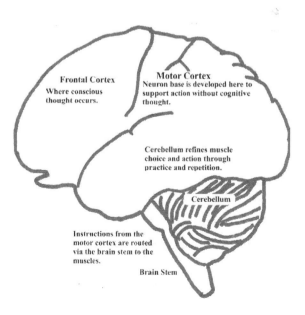

Figure 3.1 The brain

permanent state in the brain. This is like writing a document on the computer and not being able to hit save. We would have to rewrite it every day if we wanted to read it. Fortunately, our computers have an electronic chip to serve as its memory where our brains have the frontal cortex, so all it takes is the click of a button to save documents and just about anything else on our computers' memory systems. Our brains don't come with save buttons, so in order to save something into a human's frontal cortex or to the motor cortex, the human has to use whichever item or skill that needs to be saved every day over and over again, and then, after enough repetitions, or practice, the brain says, "Okay let's save," and the item or skill moves to the motor cortex and is saved in the human's memory system. Only then is it able to be called up and performed by the body without having to signal each step from the brain to the body one by one.

The skill, no matter how simple, must be repeated over and over to recruit the necessary neurons in the motor cortex to begin making them part of the permanent motor-skill base. On the day the brain finally hits save, initially only large muscles are recruited, and the action is clumsy. It takes repetition for the fine muscles to be recruited and to smooth out the performance. This process has been going on throughout each of our lives since the moment we were born all the way through learning to walk and learning to eat without assistance to driving a car. Today most of what we do is done automatically—the equivalent of these actions having been saved on the computer where it can be brought up whenever it is needed without having to rewrite or edit on a daily basis.

"The first thing we learn from studying our own circuitry is a simple lesson: most of what we do and think and feel is not under our conscious control."[28] Reading these words in David Eagleman's book, *Incognito: The Secret Lives of the Brain*, for the first time was an amazing revelation to me. To learn that I am not in control of most of what goes on in my body throughout my daily life was a bit frightening. I then learned that there is plenty of brainpower to handle the work— eighty-six billion neurons work together to carry out this responsibility. These neurons do all the things that keep us alive every day: regulating the heartbeat, taking breaths in and out, carrying on while we are sleeping, liver function, cell repair—everything! That is not what amazed me most, however. It was when I stopped to think about the enormous amount of content that we have already stored in our brains and all that we have already learned and put into our motor-skill base that are enacted for us automatically every day by our brains—all of which simplifies our daily lives considerably—that stunned me. As Eagleman says about the brain, "Most of its operations are above the security clearance of the conscious mind."[29] Each of us should just stop and think about all the things our brains do flawlessly and automatically for us every day, and then imagine how well we could play golf if we could just learn to tap into our own brainpower and let it work for us.

Finding out how my brain works made me understand why I wasn't consciously in charge of my body's daily activities—it is way too complex, and of course it makes sense that I could not possibly be able to think of every detail required to run all of its functions. We all tend to think that we have control of many more actions of our brains than we do, but it is important to remember that most of what we do, think, or feel is done for us without our conscious involvement.

Since our brains automatically operate most of our daily routines for us, we tend just to ride along without a care in the world—at least in terms of our bodily functions. Every now and then we pick up a little more information here and there and tuck it into our brains, but for the most part we run on automatic. There is a test to show us whether or not we should be in charge. I failed when I took it for the first time, even though I was totally confident that my decades of being an all-around athlete would prove that I not only controlled my actions, but that I clearly thought about how I did things. I was told to picture myself driving my car in the inside lane on a four-lane highway. There were two imaginary lanes of oncoming traffic on my left side, and one lane going my same direction to my immediate right. I was then told to imagine that I was coming to my exit and needed to get into the right-hand lane. The neuroscientist who was giving me this test asked me, "How do you steer your car from the inside lane into the right-hand lane? What actions do you take with the steering wheel? Close your eyes and say to yourself what you do." It seemed pretty simple.

I said, "I turn the wheel to the right, and then, when I am in the right-hand lane, I straighten it out and drive on." This seemed simple enough. I was certain he was trying to mess with me because I know how to drive. I waited for him to get to his point or to have him tell me that I passed this little test with flying colors, but then he told me that I had just driven off the imaginary road. "Impossible," I said to myself. "I do this every day, and I don't drive off the road." Well, of course I don't do this every day. My brain does this every day. I even went out to test the answer in my real car on a real, but quite rural, road. "Remember," I said to myself, "I turn the wheel to the right, and then, when I am in the right-hand lane, I straighten it out and drive on."

Sure enough, that neuroscientist was right; every time I did what I said I would do, I was headed straight for the curb. It's a good thing my brain knew what I was supposed to do: turn the car to the right by turning the steering wheel to the right, then *turn the wheel back to the left* just as far as I had turned to the right, and then straighten it out. My brain had put that information in the motor-skill part of my brain and saved it sometime during the decades of driving I had done prior to testing this test. I used the knowledge about changing lanes every day, but I was not required to think about it; it was saved in my brain's hard drive—the good old motor cortex. This is just one example of the many tasks the brain performs every hour of every day. We operate through skills and thoughts that are saved on our hard drives to accomplish the tasks of daily living, and this eliminates conscious cognitive processing.

Tremendous advancements in the understanding of just how the brain operates have been made since the initiative called the Decade of the Brain brought together neuroscientists, psychiatrists, and psychologists in the 1990s. Up until that time, everyone thought that the brain was hardwired, meaning that they believed that recovery from injuries to the brain was impossible and that damage caused by diseases to the brain was irreversible. Combat warriors from Vietnam proved that the old-school thinking was wrong. It took hard work for both physicians and veterans to overcome what is now called posttraumatic stress disorder. Constant repetition of desired behaviors and reactions were necessary, but retraining the brain was possible. The term plastic became the more accurate descriptive term for the brain instead of hardwired.

From the moment of our birth, our brains have been storing skills in what we might refer to as our mental tool belt. Among these skills are walking, riding bikes, swinging bats, holding hammers, using potato peelers, and keyboarding. These skills were thought to be hardwired into our brains once they were learned, but now we know they are what we call autonomous, meaning that they are performed without our having to rethink how to do them every time, and are plastic in nature and can be altered with practice. These often-repeated skills hold a priority position in the motor cortex, and, when the brain faces a new challenge, the brain quickly chooses from among these autonomous skills as its first choice for finding the skills to master new skills. That is why specific-skill sports like golf seem so hard to learn. A golfer may want to use the Vardon grip, but unless he devotes a lot of time and effort into training his brain to use this grip correctly and often enough that it becomes autonomous, his brain will choose another, more-often-used grip from his brain's established tool belt, and he will continue to hold the club with a modified broom and buggy whip grip or whichever grip is the autonomous skill.

We know for certain that the brain is plastic, and it is quite possible for a new grip to be learned and equally possible for an established grip to be changed. It just takes time and practice. To make changes in the brain, everything we do is on a trial period for seven to twenty-one days while our brain works out the kinks in the system and decides if every possible t has been crossed and every i has been dotted. It is a lot like a child learning to tie her shoes. First, she has to put her right lace over the left lace and duck it under the left and then pull. Next, she has to make a bunny ear with the new right lace and wrap the left lace around the bunny ear and the thumb. Then she has to reach through the bunny ear thumb hole and pull the left bunny ear through the hole, and finally the shoe is tied. And we think golf is complicated! The steps needed to successfully tie one's shoes have to be done over and over again until they can be performed without conscious thought just as the skills necessary for a consistent golf swing need to be repeated over and over again in order to be placed permanently into a golfer's motor cortex.

The adult brain works the same as it did when it was younger except for the speed at which skills can be assimilated into the motor cortex; it slows down as it ages. Figure 3.1 identifies the four areas that we will be concentrating on: frontal cortex, motor cortex, cerebellum, and brain stem. The frontal cortex has conscious space for about seven items at any one time, so it is critical that it is not overloaded by being introduced to several new motor skills at once. One new skill represents about 14 percent of the brain's conscious cognitive capacity, so it stands to reason that learning one new item at a time gives the brain plenty of work to do, especially if mastery is the goal. Sometimes the brain is able to draw upon parts of previously learned skills that have already been stored in the mental tool belt, which allows the brain to change what it has already stored instead of creating a whole new set of skills from scratch before turning out the desired result.

The process of learning is divided into three stages. The first is the cognitive stage. Figure 3.2 has portions of the frontal cortex shaded in black. This represents the cognitive part of the brain where thinking, remembering, and reasoning happen.

This is not where all the information is stored by any stretch of the imagination because information comes from every region of the brain when thinking happens. It travels with lightning speed to the frontal cortex where it can be available for immediate assessment. It might be fun to know that the brain is equipped to react to dangerous situations without us consciously thinking about what to do because it would take too much time for us to think of and perform life-saving actions. For instance, most people react to sudden loud sounds by ducking automatically before they have time to think about what the noise is or where it is coming from or what possible danger it means. Our brains are excellent pieces of equipment to have with us in a crisis.

Now, when we are presented with a new skill to learn, our brains will begin taking in information from all our five senses (internal) and combining that information with any instructions (external) we have received from other sources, including this book, instructors, or DVDs, and sending signals to the motor cortex, which are, in turn, sent on to the muscles, and we perform the required movements. Each skill requires a new neural pathway and millions of neurons. It is hard work and takes a lot of practice before the skill is placed firmly in the mental tool belt. Even when we are able to perform it correctly, we still do not yet own the skill. It is only stored temporarily in the memory, which is the frontal cortex, but we have not yet pressed the save button.

Figure 3.3 shows the activity in the frontal cortex sending chemically generated electric signals to the motor cortex, which will then

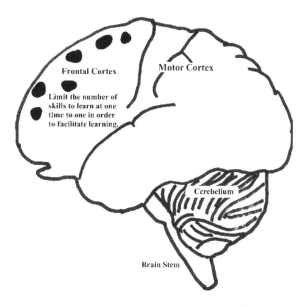

Figure 3.2 Frontal cortex working area

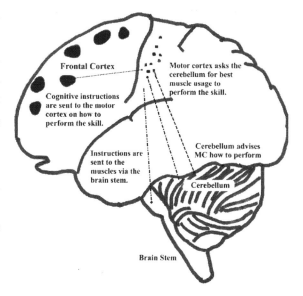

Figure 3.3 Learning process

send signals to all of the muscles required to perform the task at hand. It is necessary to remain totally focused on the one single skill we are trying to learn without trying to do too much at once or allowing distractions to occupy essential brain functioning space. Since there is limited space available in the frontal cortex, attempting to work on two or more skills at the same time will, in all likelihood, create confusion in the brain with too many signals being sent, some of which might be contradictory, and, as a result, nothing will be transferred to the motor cortex even though plenty of information is rattling around in the brain. The activity in the frontal cortex produces chemical neurotransmitters, which, in turn, produce an electric charge that connects the neurons to each other through their axons. This will eventually recruit enough neurons in the motor cortex to form a neuron bundle, and this bundle eliminates the need to remember the skill in the frontal cortex. When this has been accomplished, the skill will have been well and truly saved, just as if the save button had been pushed on a computer, and we will own the skill.

Stage two of the learning process is the associative stage. Once the brain, in the cognitive stage, has recruited the millions and millions of neurons in the motor cortex, which are necessary in order for the new skill to be performed, the skill is now well on its way to becoming permanent. Let's say that the specific skill being learned is forming a proper grip. By this stage, the golfer just has to think, "I want to form my grip," and it happens because a signal is sent from the frontal cortex to the motor cortex where the information the muscles need to perform the action is stored, which initializes the action. Only occasional mental reminders are necessary at this stage as are occasional physical checks to make certain that the action is still being performed correctly each time. In this stage, the motor cortex is now programmed. The

quality and quantity of practice during the associative stage will determine how well developed the skill becomes and how soon it is able to become an autonomous action.

During the associative process (see figure 3.4), the motor cortex, with the help of the frontal cortex and cerebellum, sorts out and recruits the various muscle combinations necessary to fine-tune the skills needed to perform the required action. The more often a golfer repeats the skill physically, the stronger the process becomes, and there is less need for any cognitive focus on the skill to complete it successfully.

This is not the end of the learning process. The associative stage can take six

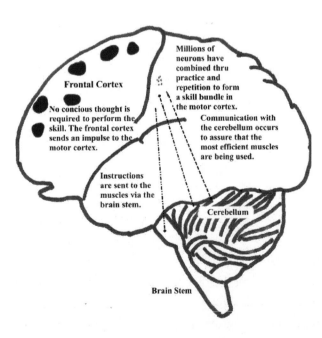

Figure 3.4 Associative process

months or longer, depending on the regularity of a golfer's practice schedule. During this stage, the golfer is developing control of the skill. Eventually, the golfer no longer needs to think about the movements involved as the skill becomes permanently stored in the brain.

There are two things a golfer can do to enhance his or her learning process:

1. Few things help anyone learn a skill more positively than teaching it to someone else. The golfer should be certain of his knowledge before he attempts this, however.
2. Once the golfer has physical control of a skill, he or she can add visualization to support the neuron base and enhance the learning process. In visualization, the golfer imagines the performance without any physical movement. This is effective in increasing the neuron base, but the student must be able to physically perform the task before visualization will be effective. (In the next chapter, readers will find more information on visualization.)

The third stage of the learning process is the autonomous stage, which can only happen after the cognitive and the associative stages have been completed. In the autonomous stage, the skills function as a unit, from the first thought of wanting to grip the club through all the sending of signals in the brain to the actual physical performance of the task. Practice is now scheduled in order to maintain the effectiveness of the skill. We continually decide how to use the skills to our best advantage by playing the game of golf. David Eagleman explains it like this: "The skills need to be pushed down into the players' circuitry. When athletes 'get into the zone,' their well-trained unconscious machinery runs the show, rapidly and efficiently."[30]

By paying attention to how we learn motor skills, we can move the fundamentals from stage one to stage three, which is the place where the physiological motor functions of everyday life live—walking, bike riding, opening doors, and all the rest of the motor skills that we use in our regular daily lives. This is where we want our golf games to be—stored permanently in our brains as autonomous actions. The acquisition of permanent new skills requires hard work and dedication; simply wishing it would happen never accomplishes anything.

Golfers who are intent upon improving their games should aim to have the fundamentals presented by the seven Legends established as autonomous actions of the brain and body. Once our fundamentals reach this level, we can begin to concentrate on the strategy of golf.

The fun begins as we continue to practice. Proper practice increases our proficiency in each of the skills that make up the fundamentals. This reduces our margins of error. Our scores begin to fall, and our confidence grows because of the predictability of the shots we make.

Once we have gained autonomous control of the skills through recruitment of the necessary neurons in all areas of the cerebrum, we can be confident that our swings will be repeatable and produce a consistent ball flight. All the various parts of the brain now work in unison to produce the best possible game for us. The neurons in the cerebral cortex, motor cortex, cerebellum, and much more are all joined with our senses to give us the best operating platform on which to base our game. The hard work we have been doing will begin to pay off!

Learning to Learn Wrap-up

1. When we want to learn a motor skill, we have to perform the skill until we own it. This takes dedication and repetition.
2. We cannot rush the process. We achieve the goal one step at a time. This means one golf fundamental at a time.
3. Each of the fundamentals may involve more than one skill, and that means learning each skill that makes up the fundamental one at a time.
4. Each skill must move through each of the three stages of learning progressively and only as rapidly as permanent learning will allow.
5. Learning requires doing; we can't think our way to a motor skill.
6. Learning begins by gathering information in the frontal cortex. Motor skill information is sent to the motor cortex and, in turn, to the muscles to perform the skills. Repetition forms neuron bundles in the motor cortex allowing us to accomplish the task. No real learning is accomplished until the neuron bundles are strong enough to create a pattern in the brain that can be followed without input from the conscious mind (the frontal cortex).
7. We walk, run, climb, drive a car, eat our meals, and perform many complicated tasks without ever thinking how we do each task. These skills are automatic, stored in the motor cortex. This is where we want the golf swing to reside. Reaching the autonomous level in each of the seven fundamentals will yield a repeatable swing with a predictable result.

4
Learning Golf

Golf is always described as a very difficult sport to learn. However, if a bunch of young boys and girls are sent out onto a driving range with a few simple instructions, they are soon whacking balls down the short grass with no problem at all. They go out onto the course, and, in no time, they are playing golf. They are having fun. Now why does that happen if golf is such a hard game to learn?

For one thing, they are kids, and they don't know that golf is supposed to be difficult. Their brains are not clogged with twenty-five different pieces of advice from buddies or spouses that make the slightest possibility of a free swing a complete improbability. Golf is difficult enough without the mental junkyard that most adults bring to the course. My advice is to leave the mental junkyard at home and focus on having fun.

Another thing that makes these kids able to perform the basic actions of golf without instruction is that they are focused on the enjoyment that comes with whacking balls great distances instead of being focused on improving their scores or their technique. Kids will naturally try different kinds of swings just to make it feel better or just to see where the ball goes next. By freely experimenting with what works and what doesn't, kids will naturally be better by the end of their first round than when they started.

Think about it, most new adult golfers are standing there on the tee about to hit their first golf ball ever, and the only things ringing in their ears are the not-so-helpful pointers they've received from some of their best friends: Keep your head down. Shift your weight. Don't swing from the top. Turn your shoulders. Don't move your head. Take it back slow. Keep your eye on the ball. Swing smooth. Follow through, and on and on. By the time they swing, they've lost a pound and a half due to perspiration, and they're beginning to doubt their sanity. What is the fun in that? My advice? Just whack it!

If a new golfer plays with golfing friends, there is a good chance that one of them will be the frustrated instructor who now believes he has 'game' and will use this opportunity to expose the uninitiated to the finer points of golf. This will prove disastrous to any new golfer. Not only will he receive more than three hours of mediocre to bad advice, but he might leave the game forever. First timers only need grip instruction and permission to whack the ball. After that, they need lots of praise for just showing up. We want new golfers to keep coming back. No one, and I mean no one, learns golf on the first day. If a new golfer hits the ball solidly on the first day—no matter where it goes—he should pat himself on the back and call it a success.

That being said, there is a distinction between playing golf and playing golf well. As golfers become more serious about improving their games, learning the fundamentals becomes more important. For that reason, and in order not to overwhelm golfers with a barrage of advice, I have tried to break down each of the fundamentals that the Legends taught into easy-to-learn skills. There are three basic types of motor skills:

1. Discrete skills are skills that have a distinct beginning and ending. These skills are often performed rapidly because there is no time for thought between the initiation of the action and the completed action.
2. Serial skills are skills that consist of a sequence of discrete actions; sometimes one of the components in the sequence might be continuous. Some of the fundamentals are a combination of discrete skills.
3. Continuous skills are skills that do not have a distinct beginning or ending point.[31]

The game of golf taken in its entirety is a continuous skill. It combines discrete and serial skills over a three- to four-hour period. However, there is a pattern for each hole that is played. The setup to hit a golf ball is a serial skill. There are several discrete skills involved in its preparation and time to think between each of the discrete skills. The golf swing would be called a discrete skill once it begins; however, it is made up of several discrete skills that make up the whole. It might be more accurately labeled a serial skill or a hybrid. The skills must be performed in unison and be executed in an exact order before the whole can be accomplished with any consistency. When a golf game is broken down into its various parts, and each part broken into even smaller parts, it is easier to master. The whole game of golf becomes more manageable to learn if a player builds his game one skill at a time.

In golf, there are no standard shots, only a series of individual challenges that use a set of discrete and serial skills to produce a cumulative score. Golf requires a mind-set that allows the golfer to adapt to changing conditions of distance, weather, lie of the ball, and time.

The last variable mentioned is time. That may be the most critical. In most sports, there is a clock that starts the game and ends it or somehow measures the performance of the athlete. In golf, there is a clock, but it is there just to make certain that the golfer does not exceed the maximum time allotted in which to make his or her shot. It prevents stalling, so golfers can slow down the rhythm of the game established by an opponent if they feel it is to their benefit. Rhythm is a critical element in sports, and, when things are going well, maintaining rhythm can be the difference between success and failure. To have an opponent suddenly slow down the pace of play can upset a player's positive surge.

We will never be able to control all the variables on the golf course, but we can prepare ourselves to face them with confidence. Building our game around sound fundamentals ensures consistency. In my examination of the teachings of the seven Legends, I have found that there is agreement among them that these fundamentals guide the play of the game. Learning the fundamentals completely, so that they become autonomous skills, is paramount. Once this has been accomplished, we must practice the fundamentals in varying conditions and in a variety of rhythms.

It is difficult to understand why the shots we have been routinely making suddenly go astray, especially just when we are beginning to think that we have the game under control. Yet it will happen. Frustration will set in as the round deteriorates and our scores soar. The golf gods—and I have admitted to a belief in them—have abandoned us yet again. Our usual response when this happens is to go to the practice range and continue to hit the same bad shots. What is wrong? The answer is simple. We have forgotten some fundamental. It is natural to think that it can't be happening, but Bobby Jones explained it this way, "Golf is a game that must always be uncertain. I don't believe that anyone will ever master it to the extent that several have mastered billiards and chess. If someone should do so, I think he would give it up—but that is a danger most of us would be willing to risk."[32]

Now, if it can happen to Jones, it can and probably has or will happen to each of us. Having strategies to deal with the results after our shots begin to fall apart is another crucial element in understanding golf. We must learn to accept the off days, use our best game, go with the fundamentals we have worked so hard to master and just play the game.

When we start to have questions about shots that go astray or when doubt creeps into our game, we need to look to our execution of the fundamentals, not to the fundamentals themselves. If our fundamentals are solid, and they can be after following the training laid out in this book, there will be no reason to look for some patchwork fix. Errors occur—practice will eliminate the frequency and the margins of our errors—but errors will occur.

There is a warning here that is worth remembering. Hitting a bad patch is not the time to go looking for something to change the fundamentals we use to play the game. Our self-confidence comes from those fundamentals. Suffering some mistakes is part of the game of golf, so when mistakes or bad patches happen, we must rely on the basic fundamentals upon which our game is built; they are our foundation. Removing a fundamental from our game once we have learned it can mean undermining that entire foundation. It is a system that will not work without each of its parts; each fundamental is vital to the whole.

Much of what we learn comes not from books, but from implicit learning: observation of others, hitting balls, continuing to play the game, and from mistakes we make. Remember that golf is an experience sport. Anyone can learn about the history of golf or learn the rules of golf by just reading, but to learn to play and play well, however, a golfer must practice by hitting lots of balls, must play regularly, and must observe others at play.

Adults no longer have to think about how to walk; they just have to know where they want to end up and the body just does the walking at the mind's bidding because those skills have become autonomous. Golf games can get to the same autonomous stage as well, but no matter how long we play or how much we practice, we never stop learning. The more often we set up the ball, look at the target, and complete the set of fundamentals needed for our swing, the more likely it will happen with fewer conscious thoughts interrupting that well-practiced swing. As we break down the swing into all its separate parts and rebuild it according to sound fundamentals using proper learning techniques, the swing will begin to happen automatically—just as we practiced it. So even though it will never be quite perfect and our game will never be 100 percent fool-proof, we can reduce the number of errors significantly, which will make playing golf much more satisfying.

There is an old Chinese proverb that says, "Learning is like rowing upstream, not to advance is to drop back." That is a good description for why we practice the game of golf. Practice is necessary to keep improving and to maintain whatever level of proficiency has been achieved. Without practice, skills will slowly erode.

I spent a lot of time in the manufacturing industry, and one of the many terms that hounded us during my tenure was the concept of zero defects—in other words, perfection. Reaching zero defects sounded great, but just how is something like that to be achieved? We were working with machines capable of producing parts to tolerances measured to within a ten-thousandth of an inch, measured by lasers, performed with repeatability that wasn't interrupted by sore or tired muscles, and controlled by unflinching computers, not brain cells subject to thoughts of disaster around the corner, and yet we couldn't reach our goal of zero defects.

The human body is not a machine, so what do we do? Errors are going to occur, and we are going to have to deal with those errors. Our brains get filled with thoughts of disaster, and we need to deal with them while our opponents are enjoying success. In the business world, we spent a lot of money and time in the areas where it would bring the most return. Similarly, it also makes sense for the golfer to invest both his money and his time in the areas in which he will get the most return in his golf game.

We need to practice the shots that will do us the most good. Making the most of practice time means dividing what limited time we have for practice among the clubs we play the most often on the golf course. If we play almost all our rounds at our home course, then we know what clubs those will be. If we have time to round out our games, then we can practice with other clubs. Most golfers will focus on the driver, wedge, and putter. We shouldn't just practice with the clubs we hit the best. To score, every golfer needs to practice his or her short game. Learning how to get up and down around the green is the quickest way to reduce one's handicap. Practice should be used wisely, devoting about 60 to 70 percent of the available time to the short game, and the remainder to hitting the driver and irons. None of us can play well if we are not in the fairway, but we will never score well if we can't get up and down.

When anyone begins learning a new motor skill, random practice is recommended. Studies have shown that random practice is the best stimulator for the brain. Random practice is practice that constantly changes the practice situation. Some golfers like to hit two shots and then change the target. Others hit two shots and then change the club. Another variation is to hit a short iron and then hit a long iron or hit another short iron and then go to a fairway wood. I like to end every practice by playing a game I call Close Out the Bag. The rules are simple; I must hit one good shot from each club, or it stays out of the bag until I do. I cycle through my bag until I get all my clubs home.

In making use of the random-practice method, golfers should change the distance and clubs frequently, which keeps practice from becoming routine. We can challenge ourselves to create excitement during every practice by setting goals, making every practice a contest, and keeping score or keeping track of how many good shots we hit in a row.

Practice should replicate as closely as possible what will occur on the golf course; this conditions the brain to the entire shot process. We do ourselves a disservice when we mindlessly whack at balls in practice without taking the time to go through the fundamental routine. Each time we address the ball, it should be as if it were the most important shot in the most important game. This is what Nicklaus did, and it worked for him. We don't get do-overs on the course, so why practice that way? Studies have shown that beginning anew with each shot, rebooting the brain, produces more positive results in learning retention in the long term.

When working on a single learned motor skill, working with a new club, or trying a new shot, block practice can be the best. Block practice is hitting the same shot repeatedly or repeating the same skill activity over and over. Repetition will not make the neuron bundle stronger unless there is something that creates excitement at the synapse. Excitement releases those chemical neurotransmitters, which help build the neuron connections. Remember, millions and millions of these neurons are needed to build a strong skill in the brain's memory system. Just as the brain can block out the repeated sounds of a highway or a train that passes by one's house at night, it will also block out the repetitive action of a golf swing unless it is accompanied by some stimulus. In order to help the brain build the neuron bundles with the correct skill being practiced, we need to keep ourselves challenged during practice to keep the very real excitement alive. Saying to oneself that it is only practice and practice doesn't matter will guarantee that the brain shuts out all the repetitive actions made during that practice session. This is the very reason why it is crucial to simulate a real golf setting for every shot made during every practice.

Spending the same time playing catch or lifting dumbbells would improve my golf game just the same if I made no effort to create excitement during my block practice sessions. I want to keep my brain actively involved by making each shot important. Merely going through my golf routine and thinking about each step is not enough. Instead, I must put emphasis on making each shot perfect and setting concrete consequences for good shots. For example, sometimes I set a specific goal. If I hit ten shots that land inside the five-foot circle on a chip shot, I get to move on, but if I don't achieve this goal, I make myself start over. Getting a partner and laying wagers always seems to help create enough excitement, even if the wagers are very small. In adding that little bit of excitement to my practices, I make each shot important. When this happens, my brain builds the correct bundles, and I am one step closer to an autonomous golf swing.

Aside from using the various practice methods described above, many athletes, including world-renowned golfers, have used visualization techniques to help their brains build autonomous skills. Two of the world's leading golfers, Tiger Woods and Jack Nicklaus, both used mental rehearsal to improve their golf games. This mental rehearsal is a form of visualization. It is a technique that gained prominence in 1984 with Russian Olympic athletes and has proven to positively impact motor-skill performance. Just how effective it can be within the context of a golf game depends on how skilled the golfer becomes in mentally rehearsing the shot he or she is about to make.

Visualization is not the same as meditation. Meditation is passive, restful, a search for peace while visualization is directed toward a desired result. Visualization is a tool used to prepare the physical capabilities held in the motor cortex to perform without interference from the conscious mind. Imagine the fundamentals: the setup, the takeaway, the backswing, the transition, the downswing, the ball impact, and the release to the follow-through. Most of all, the golfer must picture a positive result. This is the opportunity to edit the shot before it is made.

If visualization is done properly, the brain releases neurotransmitters creating the same electric signals it would have created if the body had been doing the action. Though, in this case, it is stimulated by a visualized (imagined) activity. Neurons in the motor cortex are increased and strengthened.

It is important to understand that no one can create a new motor skill in the motor cortex by visualization alone. The process is only effective after the motor skill has been physically experienced. Visualization enhances the performance of the skill and makes practice more effective.

In the book, *Neurologic*, the following are the results of a test study of four golf groups hitting balls from the sand at a flag. The visualization groups came from a mental imagery program called PETTLEP.[33]

The results of this study demonstrate that visualization did work for the golf groups tested, partly because the members of each group were experienced golfers. It demonstrated that there

Practice Group	% Change
Physical Practice	Plus 13.27
Visualization only	Plus 7.79
Visualization and Physical	Plus 22.38
Control Group (nothing)	Minus 1.94

can be improvement without the benefit of any physical practice of a known skill. The key here is that it works on a known skill; every golfer in the test groups had physically performed the skills they were visualizing prior to the actual test. While visualization does not work as well on its own as physical practice does on its own, when combined with physical practice, it has a significant additive effect. It is interesting to note the relative differences in the outcomes. Doing nothing, as the control group did, actually caused scores to get worse. Merely visualizing, without actually practicing, showed some improvement. Physically practicing showed almost double the increase that visualization alone yielded, but the combination of physical practice and visualization produced the biggest improvement by quite a margin.

"Not only can mental rehearsal improve physical performance, but it also enhances actual muscle strength."[34] The tests run at the Cleveland Clinic demonstrated that a 13.5 percent increase in muscle strength was achieved through mental rehearsal versus none for the control group and 50 percent for physical practice. It is apparent that one's imagination can make someone stronger and increase performance, which makes visualization another valuable tool a golfer can add to his golf bag.

This chapter has explained some basic learning tools. Applying them to learning golf or any other motor skill will yield success. This will not guarantee that a new champion has been made, but it will help make each of us the best performer he or she can be. There are two undeniable truths when it comes to motor skills. The first is that no one can learn motor skills faster than the brain will accept, assimilate, and produce neurons in the motor cortex. This takes time. Second, during this time, if a golfer does not practice, then any effort he has made to learn the motor skill has gone to waste. Practice has always been, and still is, the key to improvement and success.

Learning Golf Wrap-up

1. We must never give up on learning! The brain is plastic. We continue learning throughout our lives; we can learn anything, including how to play golf.
2. The Legends agree that learning the fundamentals completely, so that they become automatic, is paramount. This takes careful and consistent practice.
3. Golf is a game played in constantly changing conditions and situations. After learning the fundamentals, the challenge becomes learning to perform those fundamentals under any and every condition imaginable: changing weather, changing courses, changing the time of day, changing playing partners, changing mental attitudes, and changing any other conditions. It is important that we practice with these variables in mind.

Part III

Introduction to the Fundamentals

The minute you get away from fundamentals—whether it's proper technique, work ethic or mental preparation—the bottom can fall out of your game, your schoolwork, your job, whatever you're doing.
—Michael Jordan

The cascade of ads that promise instant success on the golf course make learning golf or improving our games sound so easy. "Change your swing in five minutes." That is a little like saying, "Learn French in one week." Our brains just don't operate that way. They can memorize, but memorizing is not the same thing as learning. Memorizing, or cramming, doesn't work when learning French, and it certainly doesn't work for learning the game of golf.

We've all seen the many offers to buy into this program or that program or to go to this school or that school; they all promise to change our golf games in whatever time we have to give—a week, a weekend. I picked up one training aid that promised to add forty yards to my drive; another claimed that with a certain wedge I would hit the ball close every time. And finally, every club manufacturer claims to have built the club with the biggest, most forgiving sweet spot and the implied guarantee that their clubs will lower every golfer's handicap. We all want a shortcut or an easier way to succeed in this game we love that adds such pleasure to our busy lives.

But the truth is simple and immutable. No one can buy a golf game. There are no shortcuts to a solid game. The only path is the one the seven Legends followed, and that path is through the hard work of learning the skills that make up the golf fundamentals. Anyone who has mastered this game has worked hard to define and refine the fundamentals through practice. The Legends believe golf is like life. Nobody learns to live life overnight.

This book has only one focus: to make each of us the best golfer he or she is capable of being while still being able to enjoy the game of golf. Not everyone is going to be the best golfer in his or her group. Not everyone wants to be or can be club champion or play good competitive golf or be a professional. But we all can be competitive, and there are very few of us who look inside ourselves and don't want to get better at the things we do. There is just something about human nature that tells us we can succeed. When it comes to learning golf, Jack Nicklaus gave us this advice. "I believe the best a fellow can do to forge himself a good golf game is to select those fundamentals that have been common to the greatest number of good players down the years, then apply them as assiduously as his talent, opportunity, and desire allow."[35] This book follows that path.

However, this book includes the fundamentals of golf, but the swing is not listed among the seven basic fundamentals. To have a repeatable, solid swing is at the heart of every good golf game, but it is merely the culmination of the other seven fundamental skills that are discussed rather than a fundamental in and of itself.

Every golfer's swing is his or her swing. It is as unique as a snowflake, and it should be. If a golfer is past the age of twenty and trying to develop a winning game of golf, he should quit looking at those picture-perfect swings that some of the touring pros possess—huge arcs, ginormous follow-throughs with pretzel-like, back-twisting finishes. Those are all well and good for someone who started playing the game in his teenage years and has always aspired to be a tour champion. Let's concentrate on the goal of this book: to develop a repeatable swing that has predicable results. If golfers can do that, they can play winning golf.

To prepare to make the swing work repeatedly, golfers should rely on the seven fundamentals. This book is meant to help all golfers learn those fundamentals and teach anyone how to apply them in the proper sequence. The fundamentals combine feel, stability, mobility, and balance. The swing can be upright or flat or in between. The golfer can be old or young, limber or stiff, thin or chunky. The swing itself can be long and flowing or short and fast. These differences really do not hinder a golfer's ability to learn and to play the game of golf. Any swing will work if it is based on the fundamentals. How well golfers develop their games depends on the amount of practice each golfer puts in and how well each one combines the fundamentals to support his or her individual swing.

The swing appears to be focused on the arms with the hands holding the club, but it involves much more than that. No matter what type of swing a golfer possesses, he must learn that all the fundamentals are involved. The swing is a rotary movement; it is a serial skill that starts from the ground up. It is initiated in the feet and sequentially moves up the legs through the hips and the torso to the shoulders and down the arms and hands to the club. All of these movements are part of the fundamentals. They all must start with the preshot routine. We will cover the basic fundamentals of the takeaway, the backswing, the downswing, and follow-through to create consistent and repeatable swings.

In learning the swing, the separate body parts must act as a unit to take the club back in a simple arc on a path inside the ball-target line and return it to the ball on approximately the same arc with the face of the club square to the ball-target line with sufficient velocity to propel the ball the desired distance. Now saying that is a mouthful. Saying and writing a description of the action is one thing; understanding it is another. Being able to perform it over and over is what golf is all about. Remember that to be successful at learning, we must think of our brains as having two separate aspects: conscious and subconscious. Thinking, remembering, and reasoning all take place in the conscious part, while the subconscious operates on its own, taking care of our heart rates, breathing, nerve action etc. without us having to think about how or when to do them.

The only way anyone can play the game with any success and hit shots under pressure is to completely shut off the thinking part of the brain and turn responsibility of the swing over to the subconscious, and that is the part of the brain that doesn't give a damn who is watching or where out-of-bounds lurks or what kind of pond sits in front of the tee or how narrow the fairway is. The subconscious only wants to connect the proper neurons in the proper order and follow the neuron paths that have been created by hitting balls during practice. If a golfer has prepared his fundamentals to act in the proper sequence, his swing will repeat that sequence and strike the ball to the best of that particular golfer's ability. Really, if we don't try to help or interrupt the sequence with conscious thought, we will strike the ball with a consistent, repeatable swing producing the desired result. Believe me, for those who learn and practice the fundamentals, golf really can be that easy.

Think of it this way. There are mechanical devices that produce repeatable swings on a regular basis, and they have no brains and no conscious thoughts to get in their way. When we practice, we recruit neurons that are schooled to reproduce coordinated muscle actions that will cause what we practiced to happen in a precise order. This action is only limited by the strength of the neurons involved and the pathways formed between the neurons themselves and the muscles. This strength relies on practice—the more practice, the stronger the neuron connection between the thought and the action. This is similar to the golf-swing machine, but it will never be a machine because we are human and, therefore, fallible. Subject to the human condition, we will not get the same response from every muscle every time our brain asks them to fire. Those neuron connections will also be subject to the conscious thoughts of the frontal cortex, which interrupt the signals. The more practice a golfer does, the more patterns he puts into his motor cortex that the muscles can follow. This is like loading a golf-swing machine. These patterns give the golfer a repeatable swing that can be adjusted to the varying conditions during the preshot routine and setup. A machine cannot do this kind of on-the-spot adjustment; it can only hit golf balls one way. It is a uniquely human ability to learn and to practice, and having a preshot routine allows us to hit balls from uneven and obscure lies in varying weather conditions, which allows us to develop a better golf game.

Hard work and successful combination of the conscious and subconscious will allow golfers to play individual games at the highest possible level. We all have days when we never want to leave the course, then others when we pray for lightning as an excuse to call it quits. When we run into a bad patch, we must concentrate on the fundamentals to get it back to the game we have been practicing. Nothing is wrong and nothing is lost when we have bad spells; we are just human. With patience, the good times will return.

Outline of the Seven Basic Fundamentals

What follows is an outline of the seven basic fundamentals that every golfer needs to know before he or she can have a repeatable and predictable golf swing. Each of these fundamentals is discussed at length in the following chapters. The fundamentals are all related to the ability to make the swing, but they are not in the chapters that relate to the swing. It is necessary for golfers to master each of the seven fundamentals before they can own their golf swings. The first of these fundamentals is the most important, and it is the grip. If nothing else is learned from this book, readers should at least master the proper neutral golf grip.

One: The Grip

The Legends all agree that this is the most neglected fundamental in golf, but it is the most important. If only one chapter is read and studied in this book, it has to be chapter 5 where we begin to build our golf game. Nicklaus started every season with a grip check. What a golfer does to make sure his grip is correct every time he takes his stance makes or breaks every shot he takes.

Figure I.1 The Vardon grip

Two: The Preshot Routine

Benjamin Franklin said, "By failing to prepare, you are preparing to fail." Failure to prepare to hit the ball happens because we don't understand the importance of all the elements of the preshot routine. Arnold Palmer suggests that we go through each of the other six fundamentals like a countdown each time we prepare to hit the golf ball during the preshot routine. Grip, stance, alignment, ball position, footwork, and rotation are like ingredients in a cake mix, and if any one of them is left out, the swing will fail. As soon as a golfer starts to pull the club back, the subconscious takes over, and it becomes responsible for continuing the footwork, rotation, and swing mechanics. Before the golfer turns the job over to the subconscious, however, he prepares himself to have the best chance possible to hit a good golf shot by creating, practicing, and implementing a preshot routine. Golf is not a static game; therefore, the swing should not start from a dead stop. This should be ample warning to all golfers to get their parts moving and be, as Sam says, "loose as a goose."

Figure I.2 The stance

Three: The Stance

The stance supports the swing, a dynamic action taking only about 1.5 seconds. The Legends caution against setting up in a rigid position that becomes static. Instead, assume a relaxed position, align you knees, hips, and shoulders to the ball-target line and keep your motionless head behind the ball; think "at ease." Relax your shoulders and stay in motion. Done correctly, a proper stance enhances the swing and improves ball striking. Snead would say, "Stay loose as a goose."

Figure I.3 Alignment

Four: Alignment

The most important element during alignment is for golfers to select a precise target every time they prepare for a shot aligning their clubfaces square to the target. The brain does not do well with generalities, so we must give it something specific at which to aim. In the mind's eye, we can draw an imaginary line from the ball to that target. Lining up the stance line and the body to this target line is essential to good shot making. We cannot be fooled by convergence and divergence.

Figure I.4 Ball position

Five: Ball Position

Where does the ball go for each club? Each golfer only has one swing. No one should have a different swing for each club. The bottom of the swing will be on a line with the instep of the front foot. The only difference in determining how far the ball will be from the body is the club length and whether or not the golfer wants to hit the ball on the upswing (using the driver), the downswing (using the short irons), or at the bottom of the swing for all other clubs.

Six: Footwork

Sam Snead would say that golfers never get too good or too old to practice their footwork. There is hardly a competitive sport played where the subject of footwork is not discussed among those who are at the top of the sport. In golf, it is a skill that comes naturally to those who learn at a

Figure I.5 Footwork

young age and is rarely paid attention to among those who learn in later life. I like to show my students how important footwork is by having them sit in a chair that swivels. I have them take their shoes off and place their feet flat on the floor in front of them about two feet apart. Next, I have them rotate themselves to the right, initiating the movement from the waist up. This is an approximation of the backswing. My students can clearly see and feel their feet working and shifting against the floor. What all golfers need to learn is what they need to do with their feet on the golf course and during practice in order to make these movements work in their favor and not against them. That is the key to good footwork. I have never seen a good golfer with poor footwork. Paying attention to the feet will significantly change the quality of any golfer's game.

Seven: Rotation

Figure I.6 Rotation

Golf is a rotary sport, and distance comes from rotation. Footwork and hip turn pull everything along. The Legends remind us that we make the backswing with the weight over the right instep and the head motionless. We stay behind the ball, shift the down pressure to the front foot, and rotate around the front leg. That is how we end up on our front heel. Golfers need to think in terms of a flexible pole running through their front side and rotating around the pole as they swing.

5
The Grip

Figure 5.1 The Vardon grip

It is impossible to overemphasize the importance of learning a correct golf grip. Each of the Legends has made a specific statement about the importance of the grip. They are in total agreement that if golfers don't have a proper grip they cannot play the game of golf to the best of their abilities. No other skill a golfer can learn in golf requires so little effort to learn and pays such huge dividends in his or her game.

Here's a sample of what the Legends have to say about the importance of the grip.

- "A correct grip is a fundamental necessity in the golf swing. It might even be said to be the first necessity, for a person must take hold of the club before he can swing it, and he must hold it correctly before it becomes physically possible for him to swing it correctly."[36] Bobby Jones
- "Good golf begins with a good grip."[37] Ben Hogan
- "It is impossible to play good golf without a proper grip."[38] Sam Snead
- "The grip…is the most fundamental, most neglected single aspect of golf. Without the right grip on the club you can practice for years, you can develop a swing that is a perfect picture of grace and balance, yet never play within many strokes of your potential best— and you will have days when you can hardly play at all."[39] Arnold Palmer
- "The grip is not the most exciting subject in golf instruction—but it is the most important."[40] Tom Watson
- "If you have a bad grip, you don't want a good swing. With a bad grip you have to make unattractive adjustments in your swing to hit the ball squarely."[41] Harvey Penick
- "…you will swing a golf club only as well as you hold it. The grip is the foundation of the golf swing. Build it solidly and there is almost no limit to how well you might play this game. Construct it poorly and, just like a house, your problems with the rest of your structure will be endless."[42] Jack Nicklaus

There is no doubt that the Legends all agree the grip is the single most important fundamental around which any golf game is built. They also agree that it is a neglected golf skill. When was the last time any of us had a grip lesson? It was so important to Jack Nicklaus that it was the first thing he did every year to make sure that he was holding the club properly before the season started. Palmer, Watson, and Snead played in numerous pro-am tournaments and remarked that, at the very least, 90 percent of the players they came in contact with had improper grips. Golfers can work on their games night and day but will continue to waste shots every time they go out onto the course because they don't take the time to correct this problem. It becomes easy to blame all errors on anything but the obvious. Until we are certain that we are holding the club with a neutral grip, we can have no idea what ball-flight problems an improper grip is causing on a regular basis. A proper grip is one where the hands oppose each other.

According to Arnold Palmer, "…only one player in fifty uses the proper grip."[43] Tom Watson has said, "…95 percent of the leisure golfers I see lack a sound grip."[44] And Sam Snead has noted that "…nine out of ten—have terrible grips."[45]

When Snead was asked to explain just how bad these grips were to the educated eye, he answered, "Their fingers resemble bananas on a vine, or snakes in a pit, more than human hands arranged to perform a delicate feat of speed and precision."[46] I would hope that by having read the quotes above and noting the tinge of sarcasm in Snead's description, readers have understood the idea that the grip fundamentals are of vital importance to the game.

Hogan offered the following corrective suggestion, "For at least a week put in 30 minutes of daily practice on the grip."[47] He didn't have the advantage of knowing about how the brain learns, but he was on the right track. In his book, he goes on to assure golfers that learning the fundamentals will be twice as easy and twice as valuable once they have a proper grip. From the chapter on learning to learn, we can confirm that this is sound advice. We learned that motor skills take between seven to twenty-one days to recruit neurons in the motor cortex, so Hogan's suggestion of spending at least seven days on practicing the skills for a decent grip were right on target.

I once had a good golfing friend ask me if it was a grip or a hold, and I answered, "It's called a grip, but we mean hold." When Tom Watson begins to explain the amount of pressure in the grip, he starts off by saying, "How firmly do you hold the club?"[48] That word *hold* has a different meaning than the word *grip*, and I have noticed that I see the Legends saying hold more often than grip. The distinction might be subtle, but worth pointing out. The definition of grip is a method to grab or hold something tightly, a strong or tenacious grasp. A hold is to have or keep in the hand, to keep fast, as in she held the purse, or he held the child's hand in his. Grip and hold suggest two different instructions, and, when applied to the golf club, have considerably different influences in the golfer's ability to play the game. Grasp is perhaps the closest synonym to hold, whereas clutch would be the nearest synonym to grip. We want to hold the club firmly, but not with a death grip. I want to put this distinction in golfers' minds from the start. We are holding and not gripping the club.

That is the message to any golf student. Nicklaus states, "I try to hold the club firmly with all my fingers, but there is obviously a stronger sense of pressure in some than in others."[49] The words used to describe the actions are important. Our brains react differently to the word grip than they do to the word hold. No one can doubt the topic in question here is the connection between the golfer and the golf club. Does it make any difference what we call it? I think it does. We know we are talking about the golf grip and that won't change, but how we describe what we expect players to do when they take the club in their hands does matter. Harvey Penick describes holding the golf club in the same terms as holding a musical instrument, and it was often remarked as he gave one of his notable speeches on golf while holding a golf club that he was doing just that—holding the club like a musical instrument.

No one can play the game of golf well without a fundamentally sound hold on the golf club. To accomplish what Snead wants us to do—"perform a delicate feat of speed and precision"—we need to be holding the club, not gripping the club. There is more to this than just studying a few pictures and grabbing the club and trying to imitate them. Holding the club requires placing both hands in the proper opposing positions with the correct pressure so that they act as one and allow the swing to flow freely with no tension so that the wrists can freely cock and uncock at the latest possible moment giving the swing maximum velocity. It is a skill. It must be learned. This skill cannot be fully learned with a tight grip on the club.

Bobby Jones said, "The clubhead cannot be swung unless it can be felt on the end of the shaft."[50] A golfer cannot feel the clubhead unless he or she has a proper grip. As students of golf develop their grips, they need to take Jones's advice and swing the club without hitting the ball just to get the feel of the clubhead. If it feels similar to the action of sweeping with a broom, the grip must be loosened. A golfer can't make shots unless he or she can feel the clubhead.

Jack Nicklaus began each season with a complete checkup from his coach Jack Grout that included a check on how he was holding the club. Jack wanted to assure himself that he was holding the club in exactly the same manner that had made him successful for years. He wanted to correct any changes no matter how slight, and he wanted to get the feel of the clubhead at the beginning of each season. "Over the years, the better I've been able to feel the weight of the club-head against the tension of the shaft during the swing, the better I've generally played."[51]

Tom Watson has always said, "You'll be amazed how lightly you can hold a club and control it."[52] It seems that everyone is afraid of losing the club. I suggest to all my students that they loosen up their grips and see how much their games improve. Loosening the grip will do two things: it will improve the ability to feel the clubhead, and it makes it easier to cock the wrists because it reduces the tension in the forearms.

Bobby Jones taught this same point in a little more analytical way: "Stiff or wooden wrists shorten the backswing and otherwise destroy the feel of the clubhead. Without the supple connection of relaxed and active wrist joints and a delicate, sensitive grip the golf club, which has been so carefully weighted and balanced might just as well be a broom-handle with nothing on the end."[53]

In forming our correct grips, let's be mindful that we are holding, not gripping, the golf club. The word *hold* describes more accurately what we should be doing. Maybe the best advice comes from Sam Snead. "Imagine that you're holding a small, fragile chicken with just enough pressure to keep it from escaping."[54] The lesson here is that tight is not right; the hold should be only firm enough to control the club as it is taken back. This will allow the wrists to cock without restriction, and, in the downswing, they will uncock naturally in a fully uninhibited swing. The grip (the hold) is then playing its designed role in the golf swing, and golfers who allow this to happen will be considerably happier with the results.

Grip Basics

Some hands have long slender fingers, some have short thick fingers, and some have medium fingers. Some have large palms, and some have small palms. So how can there be one universal grip? The simple answer is that there is not one grip that will look the same in the hands of every golfer, but there are rules that will allow every golfer to benefit from the same fundamental mechanics. Before we look at the examples of how to hold the club, let's talk about the ground rules.

We should strive for a neutral grip that is uncomplicated and repeatable. Arnold Palmer said, "There is only one right way to hold a golf club,"[55] but he allowed for three acceptable variations of that proper hold, and every golfer will fit one of them. They are all neutral: The Vardon grip, the interlocking grip, and the ten-finger grip. The best way for golfers to decide which of the three, standard, neutral grips to choose is to hit balls and find out which grip gives them the best performance.

Figure 5.2 Opposing hands

We can take this advice from Jack Nicklaus, "An effective, comfortable grip is critical in golf, so don't be afraid to experiment with different options to find the best grip for you."[56] For golfers who are just starting out, I recommend that they go to a professional or have an experienced golfing friend study the pictures of all three grips with them to help them place their hands on the club exactly like the pictures until they can duplicate the image of the hands in the grip that has been chosen.

The common factor in all three grips is they have equal pressure from both hands. Neither hand dominates. To understand this, the hands are placed palm to palm over the shaft, with one palm facing the target and the back of the other hand facing the target. The hands press together, applying equal pressure on the shaft of the club. Grip pressure should always be managed in this manner.

Grip pressure should be checked and rechecked constantly. Gripping way too tightly happens to everyone. We should hold the club in such a manner (lightly) so as not to interfere with the cocking and uncocking motion of the wrists and ensure a release. It is hard to maintain a loose grip, especially when a golfer is feeling tension. A tight grip ruins a golfer's ability to cock the wrists. It also shortens the back-swing. Tight hands equal tight arms equal tight shoulders equal a short backswing. My recommendation on grip pressure is to take a loose grip and then relax just a little. I have never witnessed anyone losing a club during the swing from grip pressure that is too light.

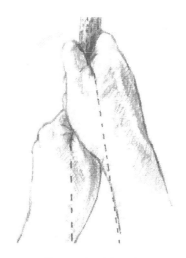

Figure 5.3 The *v*'s

Golfers should never assume that once a grip has been chosen and they have been using it for a while that it is correct. It needs to be checked constantly to make sure that the hands are kept in the proper positions. The hands work when they are in opposition to each other, and the back of the left hand is facing the target. Neither hand should dominate the grip. The *v*'s formed by the hands should point to the right shoulder and the thumbs should be placed in the proper positions, which is slightly off-center on the shaft.

I cannot say often enough that our grip is not a variable in our game of golf, so it is not to be altered during play. Once we choose a specific grip, we practice that same grip and use that same grip with every swing for every shot. We change the flight of the ball by changing our preshot routine, alignment, stance, or ball position.

As a final word about the ground rules for forming a sound golf grip, I'd like to make a distinction between supination and pronation as they apply to the hands, and more specifically the wrists, on the golf club. Almost every golf book has comments about supination and pronation. These are kinesiology terms made popular by Hogan. Let's clarify what they mean. If the hand is held out with the palm facing inward, it is in a neutral position. When the forearm rolls so the palm faces up, that is supination. If the forearm rolls so the palm faces down, that is pronation. If this hand were gripping a golf club, it would be opening and closing the clubface respectively. However, the only appropriate time for either supination or pronation is at the end of the swing as the right hand pronates and the left hand supinates to increase the effectiveness of the follow-through.

Placement of the Left Hand

In learning the golf grip, we concentrate on the top hand grip first. The top hand position, which is the left hand for the vast majority of golfers who are right-handed, is essentially the same for all three variations of the grip. The only difference in the three grips will be the positioning of the forefinger in relation to the little finger of the lower hand. The reason we concentrate on the left hand first is that the majority of grip mistakes are made with the left hand.

I cannot emphasize enough the importance of positioning the club under, and not across, the palm's heel. In figure 5.5, the grip end of the club is lying across the last three fingers of the left hand.

Figure 5.4 Left-hand grip   Figure 5.5 Under palm's heel   Figure 5.6 Across the fingers

The shaft is held with the fingers, and it rides under and not across the palm's heel. Arnold Palmer describes the correct placement of the club: "Wrap the heel pad and part of the palm over the top of the club so that your thumb points straight down the shaft."[57] He wants us to have the club locked in place. We want the left thumb pointing down the shaft just off the center line and forming a *v* with the forefinger that points toward the intersection of the right shoulder and the neck.

In figure 5.6, the club is held by the last three fingers of the left hand as they secure their hold on the shaft of the club. The thumb and forefinger will be passive in the gripping action. The three holding fingers supply pressure holding the club securely against the palm's heel. The holding power of these three fingers lock it in position and prevent it from moving during the golf swing.

Figure 5.7 Completed left-hand grip

Figure 5.7 shows the completed left (top) hand grip. Note that the club is gripped securely against and under the palm's heel. The thumb position extends down the shaft and crosses over the centerline of the shaft at the one-o'clock position. The forefinger rides comfortably under the shaft with a loose grip. The extended thumb is positioned to fit comfortably in the hollow of the palm of the right hand when it is placed on the club.

The Three Grips

There are three basic neutral grips that golfers can choose from. The size of a golfer's hands, the thickness and length of his or her fingers, and his or her age will have a lot to do with the grip he or she finds most suitable. No grip is the better choice. It will be the management of the grip that

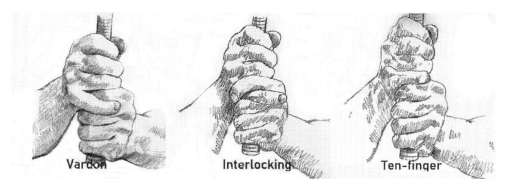

Figure 5.8 The three grips

will make it work. How did our Legends grip the club? All of the Legends referred to in this book used the Vardon grip with the exception of Nicklaus, who used the interlocking grip.

The Vardon or overlapping grip. This grip is used by about 80 percent of golfers playing today. This particular grip was popularized in the late 19th century and early 20th century by Harry Vardon, who was considered the world's best golfer in his day, although this grip was invented and first used by Johnny Laidlay, a Scottish amateur champion before Harry Vardon began using it. Sam Snead points out that taking the little finger off the club is one way that power is balanced in the grip. He theorizes that Vardon's purpose in eliminating the little finger of the right hand from the grip was to eliminate the right-hand dominance in the grip, but I could find little in Vardon's writings to support Sam's thoughts (see figure 5.9). Sam was all about being neutral in the swing. This is evidenced by Snead's swing, which is probably the most natural and smooth swing ever in golf.

Figure 5.9 Vardon grip

There are several key points a golfer must keep in mind when learning the Vardon or overlapping grip.

The hands are placed snugly on the shaft together. The palm of the right hand is perpendicular to the line of flight. The back of the left hand is perpendicular to line of flight. Remember, opposing hands have no dominant hand.

The first three fingers of the left hand are the primary grip fingers. The forefinger of the left hand only holds the club lightly.

Figure 5.10 Placement of the hands

Figure 5.11 Left thumb forms saddle

As the right hand is placed on the shaft, the ring finger slides snugly up against the forefinger of the left hand.

The pocket of the right-hand palm's heel fits nicely over the thumb of the left hand's thumb, which is extended down the right center of the shaft. The right hand grips the club with the middle two fingers. The little finger is placed in the slot between the forefinger and the second finger of the top hand (left hand for all right-handed golfers) creating a snug fit between the hands. The little finger nestles just between the knuckles of the forefinger and second finger of the left hand.

The thumb of the left hand crosses over the shaft and fits in the hollow or pocket of the right hand palm. It forms a saddle for the right hand to ride on. The middle two fingers become the gripping fingers of the right hand. The forefinger of the right hand closes loosely around the shaft. It can meet the thumb or rest closely to the thumb.

The right thumb and forefinger play little importance in the grip. When Hogan practiced, he often left the right thumb and forefinger entirely off the club.

A quick check of the two *v*'s formed by the thumbs and forefingers will show that, if properly placed, they will point at the right shoulder (see figure 5.3).

The interlocking grip. While not the most popular grip, it is the choice of two of the best players in the world: Jack Nicklaus and Tiger Woods. The little finger of the right hand actually locks into the fingers of the left hand. This is accomplished by sliding the little finger of the right (lower) hand in between the forefinger and second finger of the left hand. In doing so, the golfer creates

Figure 5.12 Interlocking grip

Figure 5.13 Positioning of right hand

Figure 5.14 Interlock complete

a secure bond between the hands. This snug fit benefits the hinging action, which is necessary to the proper release of the club.

As the right hand is placed on the shaft of the club, the little finger slides in between the forefinger and the second finger of the left hand allowing the two middle fingers to secure a grip on the shaft of the club.

At the same time, the left thumb will find a position on the shaft that is slightly off-center to the right of the shaft, and the left forefinger will find a location on the outside of the right hand.

The first three fingers of the right hand are placed on the shaft with careful attention placed on the middle two fingers. These are the gripping fingers.

The grip is completed with the thumb and forefinger closing on the shaft. The club is held by the same five fingers as in the Vardon grip and the *v*'s formed by the thumbs and forefingers point to the right shoulder.

The ten-finger grip. This grip has often been referred to as the baseball grip because it strongly resembles the grip used to grip a baseball bat and can be clearly seen in figure 5.15. It is uncomplicated, and it provides added strength for weak hands in controlling the club. It is recommended for young golfers and golfers with weak hands. Many older golfers have switched to this grip and achieved added distance. The drawback is the possible loss of control because it is more difficult to maintain unity between hands since they are simply touching and not overlapped or interlocked as they are in the other two grips. If a golfer can maintain sufficient unity between the two hands with no slippage, then he or she may find the ten-finger grip satisfactory to use.

The left or upper hand is placed on the club just as we have described earlier in this section. The right or lower hand is—and this is particularly critical—placed with the little finger snugly against the forefinger of the left hand.

Figure 5.15 Ten-finger grip

Figure 5.16 Grip unity

Figure 5.17 Ten-finger complete

In this grip, the three gripping fingers are on the lower hand. The forefinger and thumb of the left hand will be relaxed with the forefinger acting as a buffer between the two hands.

Grip Mistakes

If golfers find themselves hooking, pulling or slicing, chunking, losing distance, having no swing speed, or simply fed up with wearing out golf gloves on the palm's heel, they may have no farther to look than the grip. Sam Snead would caution that a bad grip will lead golfers to "a variety of short-term cures and compensations that cut your golfing potential practically in half."[58]

Holding the shaft across, not under, the palm's heel. The most common grip error involves holding the shaft across the palm. The grip will then rest on top of the palm's heel (figure 5.18) instead of being secured in the fingers under the palm's heel (see figure 5.19). In figure 5.18, the club extends across the palm's heel unsecured. In this position, it will shift during the backswing. Every time this occurs, the clubhead moves as well, which causes errant shots and also causes significant wear on golf gloves right on the palm's heel. Wear and tear on the glove directly over the palm's heel is a sure sign that the grip needs to be examined and corrected. Locking the shaft under the palm's heel saves money on gloves and strokes on the golf course.

Figure 5.18 Across palm's heel—INCORRECT

Mike was a student who worked hard on his game. If getting better at golf could be measured by how much a player practiced and how many balls he hit and golf gloves he wore out, Mike should have been on his way to lower scores. But for Mike, it wasn't happening. He was happy when he learned about the new glove with the extra padding right on the palm's heel. Finally, he said, manufacturers have wised up and made a glove that will not wear out so quickly. This solved one problem, which meant he didn't have to buy new gloves quite so often, but it didn't improve his golf game.

Finally, Mike and I had a talk. Mike explained that he consistently mishit his long irons, missing both left and right, and on short irons he often noticed that when he hit them solidly, they often seemed to fade. I asked to see his glove, which I clearly saw worn to

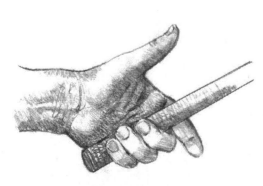

Figure 5.19 Under palm's heel—CORRECT shreds on the palm's heel. In answer to my question

whether he often wore out gloves on the palm's heel, Mike said, yes, it was a constant problem. I was able to tell him with confidence, "I think we can solve your problem."

I checked out his grip, made an adjustment, and explained to him how the handle of the club was shifting in his grip because it was not locked in under the palm's heel. One of the drills I had him do frequently is spelled out below, and Mike is a happier and better golfer today.

Figure 5.20 Mike's glove

Pronation and supination. A common mistake many golfers make is to roll their forearms during the backswing believing that it will give added power and correct ball-flight errors. It won't. Pronating (turning the wrist and hand inward from the neutral position) and supinating (turning the hand and wrist outward) the wrists and hands open and close the clubface at whatever point in the swing those changes are introduced. This means the golfer has to correct the clubhead position by returning the clubface to its starting point by the time the club impacts the ball. We do not pronate the right hand at any time during the swing except during the hitting portion of the downswing. Golfers pronate the right forearm and supinate the left forearm during the release. When the right forearm pronates, the left forearm supinates. Figures 5.21 and 5.22 show the right hand neutral and pronating.

Figure 5.21 Right hand neutral

Cupping. Golfers should never cup their wrists to get the ball airborne. The loft on the club does this for us due to its weight and design. Cupping the wrists is the more common name for what is technically called flexion and extension. Flexion and extension are terms used to describe the motion of the hands and wrists inward (flexion) and outward from the palms (extension). If a golfer's hands are extended in front of him with palms facing each other, they are in the neutral position. Pressing both hands toward the left would involve flexing the right hand and extending the left. Movement in the opposite direction would involve flexing the left hand and extending the right. Cupping is always a golfing no-no. Checking that all seven fundamentals are in order will eliminate any errors that a golfer might mistakenly believe cupping would fix.

Figure 5.22 Right hand pronating

The death grip. Gripping the club so tightly that all the muscles in the hands and arms are taut is an automatic reaction by a golfer's hands after something has gone wrong during his or her pre-shot routine. It is caused by tenseness that is created by uncertainty about the upcoming swing or putt. Something has interrupted the preshot routine. The death grip is a sign that a golfer is not ready to proceed. He should stop right there and start the procedure over from the very beginning. It is the golfer's job during the cognitive phase of the routine to give himself every chance to hit his best shot. If he is not 100 percent sure of the shot, he should not proceed. Interruptions create doubt. Doubt creates tension, and the death grip ruins shots.

To test grip pressure, golfers should swing the club back and forth in front of themselves to determine if they can feel the clubhead. If they are gripping the club too tightly, it will feel like a pole or a steel rod. All golfers should remember that when they swing their clubs back and forth, they should not cup their wrists (extending and flexing the wrists and hands toward and away from the palms); the wrists should be held firmly in the grip without any tension.

Loosening the grip and regripping. Loosening and regripping the club at the top of the swing can cause severe problems. Arnold Palmer writes in his book *My Game and Yours* that this was a problem that plagued him and was difficult to eliminate. He estimates that nine out of ten golfers will loosen their grip at the top of the backswing, and this causes the clubface to move, shifting the clubface one half of one degree or more out of square to the target line. This will move the ball as much as twenty yards left or right of the target when it finishes. This could put the ball in a bunker, the rough, the trees, or out of bounds.

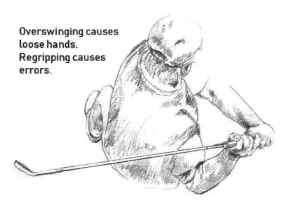

Overswinging causes loose hands. Regripping causes errors.

Figure 5.23 Overswinging

When the grip is loosened, the problem becomes regaining the grip exactly as it was during alignment, and that is nearly impossible to do. It is no wonder that so many shots are hit that do not fly in the intended direction.

The common cause for this problem is over-swinging. When the golfer tries to take too big a backswing in order to gain a little more distance, the club gets loose in the left hand. When this is happening, a golfer should shorten his backswing rather than change his grip, and increased accuracy will be his reward. The loss of distance will be slight, and the improvement in accuracy will be a significant benefit.

Using grip to correct ball-flight errors. All too often golfers use the way they hold the club to correct ball-flight errors. They do so, believing that they are going to control the flight of the ball by controlling the clubhead at impact. This is a cause-and-effect scenario. Without understanding all the causes for the ball-flight error, but witnessing the effect and reacting to it, the golfer sees the flight of the ball going astray, and, in an attempt to correct the flight of the ball, the golfer makes the one change that seems logical to him or her: he or she changes the way the club is being held. This is only a good idea if the grip is incorrect to begin with; in all other cases, the grip should not change.

Sometimes, when a golfer does change his grip, some modification of the ball flight occurs, which may seem like a correction, but no golfer would be able to repeat the 'correction' again and again. Changing the grip is more likely to add new errors, which is like putting a Band-Aid on a wound that needs stitches. That is not the way to stop the bleeding or a way to ward off infection. We don't change ball flight by changing a sound grip. The golfer should make sure his grip is correct, then check through all his other fundamentals to find the true source of the ball-flight error before making the necessary correction.

Grip Drills

Palm's heel drill. There is a drill I have all my students, especially students like Mike who are wearing out their gloves at the palm's heel, perform to practice the proper positioning of the club across the palm. For this drill, golfers should grip the club in the left hand only without completing the grip. The club should be set down as if the golfer were setting up to hit a golf ball. The first three fingers of the left hand grip the club. The forefinger and the thumb should not be involved (see figure 5.24). This drill builds a golfer's ability to control his or her grip, and having total command of the grip is the key to good golf.

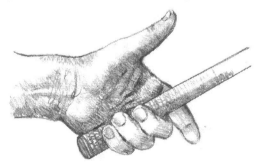

Figure 5.24 Left hand grip drill

1. The student should slowly raise his or her club until it is parallel with the ground.
2. Then he or she should count to five before slowly lowering the club. This process should be repeated five times.
3. When a golfer can successfully raise and lower the club to parallel without letting the handle roll across the palm's heel, the angle in relation to the ground should increase to 135 degrees.
4. Students should repeat the raising and lowering and counting to five at this new angle five times.
5. It is important to make sure the club is not creeping up onto the palm of the hand at any point during this drill nor should the wrists cock or cup at any point.

The Ruler or Yardstick. Sam Snead used a ruler to teach the grip to his students, and Harvey Penick used the yardstick. Golfers can use a ruler, a yard stick, or any other flat stick of approximately the same size. This is a perfect drill to do at the office or at home for golfers who have just a few minutes at a time throughout the day to practice forming a correct grip without having to get their clubs or go to a golf course.

1. The ruler should be placed in the fingers of the left hand with the flat side pressed under the palm's heel just where the shaft of the club would be. Golfers should grasp the ruler with the three gripping fingers of the left hand (not the index finger or thumb). The left thumb will naturally fall along the top, sharp edge on the opposite side of the ruler from the palm.
2. The grip should then be completed by closing the right hand over the ruler as if it were a club, making certain that the little finger is placed in the appropriate position for the specific grip being practiced.
3. When the grip is complete, the golfer should check the *v*'s formed by both hands to make sure they are pointing at the right shoulder.
4. This drill can be done as often as time allows, but golfers need to make sure to check every detail each time the grip is formed.

Closet test. I often use this with my students. I have them take their clubs into a closet or other dark space and put their full grip on the club. When I ask them to return to the light without changing the grip they formed in the dark, we can both check to see how well they have done. I am always sure to check out the alignment *v*'s with the points on their right shoulders. I continually tell these students that close is not good enough; it has to be perfect every time. In between tests, I give them at least five minutes before I let them try again.

Swing drill. This drill should be done to learn to control the club with the gripping fingers as it swings in front of the golfer without letting the club wiggle around and without cupping or cocking the wrists. It is a drill that is good for all golfers no matter their level of proficiency since controlling the grip is the key to a solid and repeatable swing.

1. Using a six iron, the golfer should grip the club using only the last three fingers of the left hand and the middle two fingers of the right hand. The other fingers should hover just above the shaft, but not play a part in actively swinging the club. In a regular swing, only the first five fingers mentioned should control the swing, even though in a full-out swing the other fingers are wrapped around each other or the club in various ways when forming the three grips.
2. Using a shortened backswing, the golfer should hit several balls, going through a full preshot routine for each swing.

3. Golfers should watch to make sure the knees are slightly bent, only the arms are moving back and forth, the wrists are not cupping or cocking, and the head remains looking at the ball.

4. The golfer should not overswing; he or she should just make a smooth swing and concentrate on keeping the correct grip throughout. The golfer should check every detail of the grip before going through each preshot routine.

5. As confidence grows, the golfer should let his or her swing path grow. If the club cannot be controlled throughout this drill, it is an indication that the golfer is hitting at the ball rather than swinging through it.

Visualization. Practicing the grip is the ideal place for golfers to put their mental skills to work. We all need to remember that we have to learn the grip fundamentals first before we can use mental and visual imaging to improve the grip. However, once a golfer has performed the grip repeatedly and correctly, using visualization can help train the brain to move the process from the conscious part of the brain to the subconscious (see chapter 3).

The Grip Wrap-up

1. The Legends are unanimous in stating that the grip (hold) is the most important fundamental in the game of golf. The hold on the club is our only connection to the ball. It should be obvious that we cannot play good golf without knowing how to hold the golf club properly. A proper hold on the club is neutral and will not affect the flight of the ball.

2. The grip is not variable. It is neutral and remains the same for every club—possible exception is the putter.

3. The club is held, not gripped. If we cannot feel the clubhead, we cannot play the game to our full potential.

4. The hold must allow the swing to flow freely with no tension so that the wrists can cock and uncock at the last possible moment.

5. The club is held by the fingers and locked into position under the palm's heel of the left hand.

6. Golfers should not loosen their hold and regrip the club at the top of the backswing. This is a fatal flaw.

7. In positioning the *v*'s, remember that the left-hand *v* is pointed toward the intersection of the neck and right shoulder, and the right-hand *v* is pointed toward the intersection of the right arm and right shoulder.

8. In the grip, neither hand is dominant. The back of the left hand and the palm of the right hand both face the target.

6
The Preshot Routine

The difference between a sand trap and water hazard is the difference between a car crash and an airplane crash. You have a chance of recovering from a car crash.
—Bobby Jones

The goal of this book is to help golfers achieve a repeatable swing with a predictable result. To reach that goal, I have taken the dominant teaching lessons from seven Legends of golf and matched and consolidated them into one teaching tool that I hope will convince readers that the wisdom gleaned from decades of golf knowledge is available to us without our reinventing the game or applying new math or twenty-first-century technology to our learning efforts.

The Legends urge us to begin where they began and progress from there, so let's continue to learn the game of golf. The Legends agree that two of the most critical parts of any teaching series should be the grip and the preshot routine. They are emphatic about the necessity of a sound grip and the need to learn both how to form the grip and how to practice the grip until it becomes second nature. After a golfer's grip reaches the autonomous stage, it must be checked frequently to make certain that no deviations, however small, in the way the hands are placed on the club have crept into it. Over time, the hand positions on the club can change, and these changes, no matter how minor, can affect the position of the clubface at impact. Using cruise control on a long drive versus controlling the speed manually is an excellent real-life example of how subtle changes creep up on us. Which is more exact: the electronic cruise control or the pressure our foot exerts on the pedal? Of course, the machine is more exact, so when we use our foot, sometimes we find ourselves going just a few miles above or a few miles below the speed we are trying to maintain. Yet we feel no perceptible change in our speed; we must constantly check the speedometer to make little adjustments as we travel. We check our grip repeatedly for the same reason.

We learned the grip first because it is the most important fundamental. It is our connection to the club, and our grip establishes our feel for the game. The preshot routine is the procedure that combines the grip with other fundamentals. We must think of it as a preshot checklist that must be completed before we strike the ball. Arnie explains it this way: "Address is the position a golfer puts his body in before making a swing. The address 'sets the table,' so to speak, for a good swing motion to occur."[59] Arnie's description may be old, but it is accurate. Setting the table, addressing the ball, the setup, and the preshot routine are all terms that refer to what a golfer does before he actually strikes the ball. This preparation before the swing is every bit as important as everything else that will be learned about the rest of the game.

Here is why. In the introductory quote for this chapter, Bobby Jones describes one of golf's greatest difficulties: consistency, which is the ability to hit even the simplest shots correctly over and over again. Why we can't do it is not a great mystery. The golf swing is full of variables, and when we list them all, it seems most improbable that we are able to navigate through that minefield of potential mistakes successfully as often as we do. We all flub easy shots that we are accustomed to making, and it's more or less reassuring to read the words of a golfer of Jones's stature revealing that he has had the same problem.

However, that does not provide a solution. To fight against this problem, each one of the Legends established a routine that he did prior to each shot. They each followed this routine in order to be confident that each of the necessary preshot fundamentals was completed prior to starting the swing. This was to ensure that a consistent swing would continue producing a predictable result. The importance of the setup is the second universal agreement among the Legends, and it is a combination of several fundamentals. From Jones to Watson, all seven of them had a specific method of preparing to hit the golf ball, none perhaps more specific than Nicklaus.

Jack Nicklaus often wrote of the importance of the preshot routine. In his book, *Golf My Way*, Jack wrote a chapter titled, "Setting Up: Ninety Percent of Good Shot-Making." In his 2002 book, *My Golden Lessons*, Jack again stressed the setup stating that he had "said and written many times over the years that golf is 80 percent setup."[60] From Jack and the other Legends, we learn that the preshot routine is not just getting ready to strike the ball, it includes important fundamentals. Ignoring any one of the setup fundamentals makes playing consistent golf impossible.

Nicklaus went through his complete routine every time he hit the golf ball—not just in competition, but every time he hit the golf ball. His preshot routine was a habit fixed in his brain; "I never hit a shot, even in practice, without having a very sharp, in-focus picture of it in my head."[61] Nicklaus knew the true meaning of the statement that there are no casual shots on the golf course. In our game, no do-overs are allowed.

The questions I hear most often from amateurs are why is there this need to be so exact? If there is something I am missing, why haven't I been told more about this and its importance to my game? Let me explain. The problem most golfers have is that we are not accustomed to doing things that are so precise in any other area of our lives. Precision has been put into the hands, if you will, of technology. All we need to do is to sit in front of the computer and wait while a program does the hard, exacting work of installation and configuring the hardware or software, or watch as the latest app takes care of the details for us. Golfers do not have the luxury of that kind of passive involvement during the setup for a golf shot. In golf, the golfer gets one chance to prepare for the shot. Preparation dictates the outcome.

In most other daily activities when things are being set up, there always seems to be some give-and-take or some sort of negotiation. If something is left out of a home improvement project, there is usually some chance to fix things before the results are final. In any other sport, there is ebb and flow that exists allowing for errors to be overcome before the results are final. For example, there are four quarters in a basketball game during which players can score additional points or increase defense to even the score. A lot happens in the second half of a football game. Likewise, in business, the setup or preparation for negotiations can take place over days or maybe weeks, and the event can take equally long to come to completion. This is not true in golf. Being surrounded by these and other similar situations, we get the idea that setting up for a golf shot does not have to be so precise. But it should be, and it should be true for every shot. Once the swing begins, the result is known in less than one and a half seconds. It's over and done with. Another stroke is added to the score sheet.

The golfer is alone when he or she gets ready to hit a golf ball. Once the takeaway begins, there is no chance to correct what he or she has put into motion. Brain studies tell us there is no real possibility that once the swing starts a golfer can have a conscious thought and put it into action to correct what has been put into motion. There simply cannot be new thoughts to redirect the motor skills in order to achieve a successful outcome. There is not enough time. The result, good or bad, is dependent on the preparations that have been made during the preshot routine. The only help a golfer can give his swing is to try not to interrupt the flow with conscious thinking once the action starts. A golfer might be able to stop the action, but he can't correct it. There are no delete or refresh buttons for golf swings.

A golf club travels seventy to more than one hundred miles per hour into a very short hitting zone, which is where the face of the golf club must be square to the target line. The preshot routine is the only time a golfer has to allow the brain to put into use what it knows about golf. Once the swing begins, none of us can consciously think our way to better results.

The why question now seems easy to answer. Let's jump ahead and imagine the best possible swing on a golfer's best day. That is the swing we want to capture and keep. It's the swing we want to hit most frequently on the driving range, and it should be our practice swing. It's the swing we hit balls with when the shots don't count. It's the swing we use with our favorite club. It is the swing we want our brains to store in a bundle of neurons and hold on to tightly so that we can reproduce it every time we swing the club at a golf ball. Hooray! Another predictable result. We are now playing good, or maybe even great, golf.

What many golfers may not understand is that the perfect swing and ball strike don't happen without a perfect—and I do mean perfect, or as close to perfect as a human being can get—preshot routine. Some days we get lucky and get in a groove and, without really thinking, we manage to do everything just right. But unless we absolutely know what we are doing and remember to do

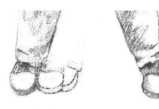

Figure 6.1 Stance narrows as clubs get shorter

it every time we set up to the ball, we are just guessing. In golf, when we guess, our game is a crap shoot. We must practice every move that leads up to that swing over and over again if we want to reproduce that swing when it really counts.

Once golfers develop that repeatable swing, it will be the only swing they ever need. We use the same swing with every club in our bag. Nicklaus said it this way: "Get it out of your head—if it was ever in there—that you deliberately have to make a different kind of swing with each club. Certainly in terms of plane, you should feel like you are making the same basic swing with every club in the bag (except, of course, your putter). Whatever differences do in fact occur will do so automatically as a result of shaft length. Your arc decreases with the shorter clubs, and your plane becomes more upright as, of necessity, you move closer to the ball."[62] The shorter the club, the narrower the stance.

If we have this repeatable swing, what determines the distance and direction of the ball? It is all very simple: the distance, trajectory, and direction are based on the club that is chosen and the soundness of the preshot routine. There is only one grip, one preshot routine, and one swing. None of us should swing differently for variations in external conditions. The outcome of each shot depends on several different things. The grip, stance, ball position, and alignment are all critical fundamentals and skills that golfers must have mastery over in order to prepare the setup prior to swinging the golf club. These are all things every golfer should check before he or she swings and are necessary in order to perform consistently. As Jack Nicklaus says, "…the better you want to play, the more attention you must pay to what you do before you ever swing the club."[63]

Right along with correctly forming and checking and rechecking a proper, neutral grip, golfers should note that the loft and length of the club determine trajectory and distance.

The position of our feet, hips, and shoulders are established in our stance. This is all a part of alignment and aids in rotation for increased distance.

Noting the position of the ball is next in line when we establish our preshot routine; ball position is a fundamental and must be checked and rechecked along with the other fundamentals. We must ask ourselves if we will hit the ball on the downswing in a descending strike, on the level at the bottom of our arc in a sweeping strike, or on the upswing just past the bottom of the ascending arc. These strike points all have to do with the arc of the swing of the golf club. We make no changes in our swing to achieve any of these hits on the ball. The only variable is whether we hit the ball earlier or later in the swing arc.

Alignment is relative to the direction of the swing. Our shoulders, hips, and knees are all parallel to the ball-target line, which is the direction we want to swing along.

Golfers will have to understand each of these elements completely, or our game will let us down. Without mastery of each of these elements, we can't set up properly, and if we can't set up properly, we are leaving the result to chance.

Legends Nicklaus and Watson often gave clinics together, and, during one of them, Nicklaus said to Watson, "If you have a proper grip and proper setup, you can be taught."[64] Fellow Legend, Sam Snead, stressed how to set up and aim correctly in his chapter of the same name in his book *Sam Snead Teaches You His Simple "KEY" Approach to Golf*. To Sam, this meant focusing on balance for consistency and by hitting the ball at the lowest point or slightly before the lowest point in the swing arc. Sam wanted the clubhead traveling forward in the hitting zone and having the swing arc coincide with the ball-target line. Snead tells us that he would set up and then put his body on automatic pilot; before he hit, he felt like "…my mind is blank and my body is loose as a goose.[65]

Snead gave us a look at his visualization process, which he labeled blueprinting. In order to blueprint, a golfer needs to know his game, both strengths and weaknesses. If a golfer knows his swing, then he can blueprint a course and a plan of action for his round of golf. "You can actually 'blueprint' your round and save innumerable shots which you ordinarily would throw away if you gambled needlessly or tried hitting risky shots."[66] To put this to work, we should follow Snead's outline.

First, golfers should plan the course according to the weather and aim their shots at targets that can be hit eight out of ten times. Golfers should visualize themselves playing the course for position, not for a score, which will give golfers confidence.

Second, golfers should visualize their swings from start to finish, and if there is a problem, golfers should try to fix it by envisioning it better.

Third, we need to visualize the shot we are going to hit—the flight and the landing. Sam Snead said, "I always tried to picture each shot I hit before I hit it. Then it seemed as if I didn't have to think about it consciously when I got up to the ball."[67]

When we work hard to develop a golf game, we need a method to put what we have learned into action. The best golfers there have ever been learned that to succeed they needed a preshot routine. Harvey Penick explains it this way, "You just have to take the attitude that you have done all the training that is required, and if you are not going to trust it, why do all the training?"[68] It is time to put a method to work that will allow us to turn our swings over to our subconscious.

Just imagine, the secret to what is described as one of the sweetest swings ever, Sam Snead's, is not to think while swinging and that the greatest golfer among the Legends, Jack Nicklaus, never hit a shot without his preshot routine. The Legends as a group advocate preparing for each shot as if it is the only one that counts. No matter what we do in practice or in play, it all starts with the preshot routine.

Since we have been stressing the importance of going through a very specific preshot routine for every single shot we take, perhaps it would be best to set out each step to take in creating a preshot routine in the form of a checklist that every golfer could follow while checking his or her own personal grip, stance, ball position, and alignment. Here is the checklist for the preshot routine preparations:

1. Golfers should approach the ball from behind and evaluate the terrain, lie of the ball, and identify a specific target to determine what shot they can play. All golfers should visualize the shot in detail before doing anything else.
2. The next step is to determine alignment by identifying the ball-target line. Golfers should pick out an intermediate target about twenty-four to thirty inches in front of the ball that is in line with the target. This will aid in establishing the ball-target line as golfers move to the side to prepare to hit the ball.
3. Selecting the best club for the shot is the next thing golfers should consider. They should make practice swings with the same swing that they will use to hit the shot.
4. Once the first three steps are completed, the golfer should move to the side of the ball and set the clubface behind the ball on the ball-target line and square the clubface to the ball-target line. This is done by putting the left hand on the club. With the clubface now perpendicular to the ball-target line, golfers should set their right hands on the golf club to establish a proper grip.
5. The golfer's left foot should be set first to establish the distance and ball position and then his right foot should be set on a line parallel to the ball-target line. The placement of the front foot is critical in establishing the proper ball position and hand position. (Chapter 9 discusses ball position.)
6. Golfers can complete their stance by bending their knees and bending forward from the hips (not the waist), shoulders relaxed with right shoulder lower than left, back straight, arms hanging freely in front of the chest, weight equally on insteps, right knee pointed in toward the ball, and the hips aligned according to the terrain. (Chapter 7 discusses stance.)
7. Golfers should make certain their knees, hips, and shoulders are square to the ball-target line. (Chapter 8 discusses alignment.)
8. Keeping the head still and behind the ball is crucial. This is an absolute key to good ball striking and is emphasized by each of the Legends (see chapter 7).
9. The final step is for each golfer to create his own mantra. This is a short phrase said mentally that releases the conscious brain and turns over the action to the motor cortex. The subconscious then takes over. It is a golfer's way of releasing mental control. No thinking should be needed after this point; all the preparations have already been made. The golfer will have to use the phrase on the practice tee and prior to every shot ever taken in order for it to be effective. As Snead said, "Be loose as a goose." When no conscious thoughts interrupt our actions, we can and will play our best golf.

In order to improve or to learn the game, golfers will have to develop a preshot routine and stick to it. This routine must become a habit. To Jack Nicklaus, mental preparation as well as physical routine was a part of his setup. Considering that Nicklaus must have hit as many practice balls as Sam Snead, we can easily imagine Nicklaus going through his setup routine more than one and a half million times while practicing. We now begin to understand how greatness is developed.

Preshot Routine Wrap-up

1. To perform a repetitive swing, we should not interrupt the swing action with conscious thought. We must allow the motor cortex to perform the swing that we have been practicing for the shot we have chosen.

2. The Legends each followed a preshot routine so they were confident that each of the setup fundamentals was complete prior to starting each swing. This was to ensure a consistent swing that produced a predictable result.

3. Golfers should make the setup routine a habit. Nicklaus tells us to use the setup routine in practice—always.

4. Nicklaus went through his routine every time he hit a ball whether in practice or in play. We can imagine that Nicklaus hit as many balls as Sam Snead, and based on the fact that Snead hit one and a half million golf balls, we can imagine that Jack did likewise. That would mean that he went through his routine more than one and a half million times. That is the source of greatness.

7
The Stance

The stance is often thought of as a static position that supports the golf swing. Our Legends caution against the idea of setting up in a stance and becoming static rather than dynamic. The stance should be defined as a preswing position because if it does not facilitate the golf swing, it has no value. The swing is a dynamic movement lasting only part of two seconds from start to finish, and a golfer's stance is a support position or fundamental made up of several discrete skills. There are many possible errors that could occur while establishing a correct stance, any one of which would prevent a golfer from achieving a successful swing. Done correctly, a proper stance enhances the swing and improves ball striking. If we went to the Legends and asked them what are the keys to a good stance, what would their answers be?

Figure 7.1 The stance

- Harvey Penick: "Before you can stay behind the ball, you must get behind it. I mean set up with your head behind the ball and keep your head behind the ball."[69]

    The Legends agree, and not only do the Legends want us to set up with our heads behind the ball and keep it there, they want us to keep it motionless. This was one of the very first places they looked when errors started to occur in their games. Head movement is a killer.
- Bobby Jones: "The keynote of the address position should be ease, comfort, and relaxation."[70]

Figure 7.2 Behind the ball

    If a golfer has tension in his setup, it is contrived, and muscles don't function as well as they should. When we make our practice swings, we are nice and relaxed. This is the same swing we should use to hit the ball. If our setup involves

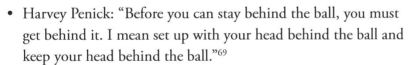

tense muscles, we cannot swing loosely. A golfer's arms should hang loosely from his shoulders to allow for a free-swinging motion across the chest.

- Jack Nicklaus: "Maintain your weight on the insides of your feet at address, on the backswing and at least through impact…"[71]

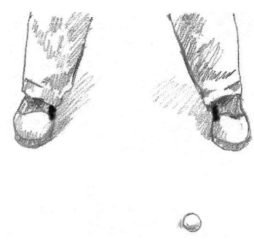

Figure 7.3 Weight on insteps

Keeping the weight on the inside of the feet is the key to maintaining balance throughout the swing. When the foot rolls over and the weight goes to the outside, golfers lose their balance. The brain makes automatic corrections, and the golfer loses control of his swing. The position of the feet for the driver must be made with the feet wide enough (just wider than shoulder width, but not more than one shoe width wider) to give the golfer a rock-solid feeling. All adjustments for stance width for other clubs are from the driver stance. A golfer should reduce his stance one shoe width for fairway, utility woods, and midirons and reduce it another one-half shoe width for the more lofted irons. A wider stance produces a stronger base and therefore a more stable base for the golfer. His balance is also increased by keeping his weight focused on the insteps of his feet both in the backswing and in the downswing. It is only in the follow-through of the downswing that the front foot allows the weight to move across the foot to the front side and eventually to the heel.

- Tom Watson: "Flex your knees slightly, and kick your right knee in toward your left knee to help brace on the inside of your right foot on the backswing."[72]

When a golfer flexes his knees, he drops his center of gravity. This should be a slight flex; the golfer should be balanced, not squatted. Nobody can rotate effectively from a squatted position. The golfer should have a forward tilt from the hips and a bend at the knees. The back should be relatively straight from the buttocks to the neck in order to make the necessary rotary movements with the core portion of the body.

- Sam Snead: "The best golfing stance to start with is a 'comfortably square' stance such as mine, with shoulders and feet set on a line that is close to parallel to the target line."[73]

Snead believes that it is easier for beginners to have the feet square when they are learning the game and then to modify the foot position as they get more comfortable with alignment. Snead's advice is to learn to swing square to start, and this is easier done with the feet square to the ball-target line. Arnie hit all his shots this way.

- Ben Hogan: "The proper stance and posture enable a golfer to be perfectly balanced and poised throughout the swing."[74]

Balance is established by maintaining the weight on the insteps of the feet. The weight should not shift to the outside of the feet either in the backswing or the downswing. If a golfer finds himself on the back foot and off balance at the completion of his swing, then he knows right away that his stance is incorrect. If this is happening, then the golfer is not getting maximum performance out of his golf swing. If he starts out with a proper stance, but ends up out of balance, then he is overswinging, making an improper weight transfer and follow-through, or not rotating. Golfers should stop and review their backswing and downswing fundamentals to make certain they understand where exactly the problem originates. Loss of balance means loss of strokes.

Figure 7.4 Stance position

Palmer has already told us that the setup was like setting the table, and the stance is but one of the elements. Each of the elements requires certain skills, and, as Jones advises, being in a relaxed position helps produce the necessary stability. Physics research tells us that stability can be further enhanced by lowering the center of mass. Following Watson's advice, we bend at the hips, but we do not crouch. This would impede our golf swing. If we bend too much, we limit our arc, and this limits our ability to generate clubhead speed. Our back needs to be relatively straight to turn or rotate. Our hips and shoulders are key to the golf swing. We need to find a satisfactory compromise that creates stability, provides for the necessary balance, and allows rotation of the core so the arms swing freely. The stance position as shown in figure 7.4 accomplishes those requirements.

A golfer's balance should be as perfect as possible especially when swinging a club at speeds in excess of one hundred miles per hour and hitting a small white object. If the golfer is not in a balanced stance, then hitting that golf ball consistently is an impossible task. There is a finite point located inside the body called the center of mass (COM) (figure 7.5). In the golf swing, it is located approximately at one's sternum. For the brain, this point determines where everything is in equilibrium. It is also referred to as the balance point. The brain uses this reference point to make adjustments in order to keep the body in balance.

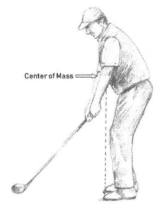

We have a finely tuned system made up of muscles, bones, and tendons that is controlled through a system of signals to the brain from all our senses, the inner ear, and senses in the body (such as the skin, the muscles themselves, and joints). This balance system is also known as the vestibular system. The inner ear has the semicircular canals filled with fluid and hairs that tell us where we are in space and how we are moving.

Figure 7.5 Center of mass

Figure 7.6 Motionless head behind ball

Signals from these various systems are sent to the brain, which sends corrections instantly to the muscles so the body maintains its balance. This is done without input from the cognitive part of the brain. We do not have to think to maintain our balance; our brain will make corrections for balance automatically during our swing. This ability to remain upright without conscious thought is an excellent asset, but it can cause errors in our shots. This is why it is necessary that we practice.

A proper golf swing begins with coiling the torso (rotation) in a clockwise manner, which builds torque from the ground up, and that torque is unleashed in a counterclockwise movement, again from the ground up, to add power to the swing. If we do not have a proper setup and have not established a solid base, we will not be able to coil and uncoil the torso (rotate) properly and maintain balance. This will cause the brain to correct the balance problem automatically no matter how slight.

The most frequent error is head movement. This causes problems with the swing arc and swing path of the club and the direction of the ball flight. The reminders echo throughout the teachings of the Legends that a motionless head is a necessity for consistent ball striking. When things started going badly for any of them, it was one of the first places they looked for a cure.

Beginning in the backswing, we shift the weight from a balanced neutral position, which has the weight on the insides (the insteps) of both feet during the preshot to the inside of the rear foot, and then shift to the inside of the front foot to begin the downswing. This movement affects the location of the golfer's center of mass. The COM stays inside the stance, but moves from center to the right and then to the left. The head must remain the anchor point and stay motionless. The COM shifts from the center of the body to the right side of the body during the backswing and then to the left side during the downswing. The golfer manages the COM by managing his weight on the insteps of his feet. His balance is also increased by keeping his weight focused on the insteps of his feet both in the backswing and in the downswing. It is only in the follow-through of the downswing that the golfer allows the weight to move across the front foot along its front side and eventually to the heel. Remember the COM is not static. When the golfer moves, even slightly, the COM moves, and the body will move to adjust for it automatically.

A golfer's proper stance will allow him to maintain his balance and keep his head relatively motionless while he rotates his torso clockwise and then counterclockwise, ending up on the left side. All this time, the brain is going to be correcting for this movement without considering what it does to the arc of the golf swing. These minor balance adjustments during the swing could take the golfer off the ball-target line, cause him to hit behind the ball, top the ball, or change the swing path. All the Legends worked hard to train their bodies to maintain a balanced position during this movement.

When we watch a dance troupe perform or a military unit on a parade field, we learn to appreciate uniformity. In establishing a golf stance, uniformity is not necessarily the key. Everyone is built slightly differently, so each stance will be unique to each golfer. There is, however, a right and wrong way to stand. All golfers need to learn the functions of the stance.

We begin by describing the stance as the swing position. The purpose of the stance is to facilitate a very dynamic movement—the golf swing. If the stance does not do this efficiently, it is not an effective stance. The swing movement lasts only part of two seconds, but this support fundamental is made up of several discrete skills, and there are several key potential mistakes that could prevent a golfer from achieving a successful swing. If it is done correctly, a proper stance can enhance a golfer's swing and improve his ball striking. A proper stance

1. prepares the golfer for the footwork involved in the swing;
2. positions the hips, torso, and shoulders to allow for proper rotation;
3. allows the arms to swing freely across the chest; and
4. establishes a position that will allow the golfer to maintain balance.

It accomplishes all the above and is not a contrived position. This is stressed by all the Legends and summed up best by Harvey Penick: "Be comfortable and at ease, not straining anything."[75] Here is a piece of advice from Jack Nicklaus: "When a soldier standing stiffly at attention is given the at-ease order, the first thing that happens is a slumping of the shoulders. 'See' and feel your shoulders behaving just like the soldier's as you set up to each shot, both in practice and in play."[76] If golfers allow themselves to slump or relax as they set up, it will aid golfers to achieve the best results during the full swing.

Being relaxed in the stance promotes that key ingredient called balance. Balance is enhanced when no tension exists. Simple physics research tells us that we could create greater stability by widening our stance and lowering our center of mass, but we cannot be effective ball strikers.

Any athletic endeavor requires balance. Maintaining balance while swinging the golf club is essential to bringing the clubface back to the ball squarely in line with the intended line of flight. On longer shots, a one-half-degree error of clubface deflection can cause as much as twenty yards of error in the line of flight. Sam Snead recognized this and wrote that the purpose of the stance is to enable a golfer "to achieve consistency through balance…."[77] In his opinion, this could be achieved only through a fairly upright stance. He goes on to say, "…if you crouch too much at address, you'll tend to straighten up during the swing and alter the line along which the club head is moving. If you stand too straight, you'll tend either to crouch or to fall back as the action develops."[78] The body's effort to maintain balance is involved.

Our Legends definitely have strong opinions when it comes to the golf fundamentals. Palmer expressed his opinion that there was only one grip, and we had to agree that he was basically correct. Agreement on stance among the Legends is a bit more varied; each golfer will need to take the information below and find what works best for him or her, what seems most comfortable, and what produces the best results.

- According to Hogan, "…there is one correct basic stance: the right foot is at a right angle to the line of flight and the left foot is turned out a quarter of a turn to the left."[79] Figure 7.7 shows the foot positions for the Hogan stance. Hogan's right foot is positioned at a right angle to the line of flight or ball-target line in order to restrict the rotation of the hips during the backswing. Hogan felt that by turning the right foot out and thereby having "the incorrect positioning of the right foot can lead to many serious errors, including dipping the left knee, swaying the right leg out to the right, turning the hips excessively, and making a forced, incorrect shoulder turn as the left arm breaks…."[80] Hogan's left foot was more open as the clubs got shorter and more closed as the clubs increased in length.
- Nicklaus kept his right foot at ninety degrees with every club except the driver. When he did use his driver, he slightly turned the right foot out approximately ten degrees. His left foot placement was approximately like Hogan's.
- Watson prefers to stand up to the ball with both feet open. Hogan would take exception to this stance. His right foot is ten degrees open matching how Nicklaus stood when he drove the ball, but Watson did this with every club. Watson then placed the left foot twelve degrees open on every club (see figure 7.8). He believes this facilitates the core turn in both directions.
- Palmer lined up with everything square to the target—both feet at ninety degrees to the line of flight. Palmer was square to the target line throughout this stance with knees, hips, and shoulders.

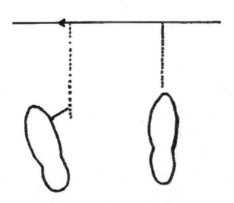

Figure 7.7 Hogan stance

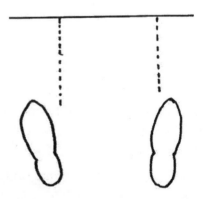

Figure 7.8 Watson stance

- Snead teaches us to stand square to the line of flight when developing our swing, but after the swing has been developed, golfers can take a more relaxed stance. His stance in all respects is more like Watson's stance with both feet open slightly.
- Harvey Penick advocated that above all else any golfer should be natural, almost casual, about taking his stance. He felt that the Hogan stance was a good place to start with the right foot at ninety degrees, which kept the golfer from overturning during the backswing, but he was not against having the right foot turned slightly open allowing for more turn.
- Bobby Jones had the most upright stance of all our Legends. His feet were closer together, and he had both feet turned slightly out—the right foot only about ten degrees and the left a full quarter turn or twenty-two degrees open.

The consensus seems to show that Hogan's assertion that there is only one way to stand is incorrect. There can be slight variations of how to place the feet. However, what we do get from our Legends is that consistency is important. Each one of them stressed that the swing begins from the ground up. We can surmise that we need to have our feet in the same place for each club so that our swing arc will be consistent.

Since the stance is a major fundamental, it should be learned and practiced until it becomes automatic, just like the other fundamental skills we've discussed. The elements of the stance not only contribute to the swing, but also enhance a golfer's ability to maintain balance during the swing. As we have discussed, balance is key to accuracy in all our golf shots, and paying close attention to how the body parts work together guides us toward achieving comfortable balance.

The Stance Wrap-up

1. The stance must be established to facilitate repeatable movement. It is not a static position; golfers should stay loose and flexible.
2. In order to hit the ball consistently, we must be behind the ball. It is important that we set up with the head behind the ball and keep it there until the ball is struck.
3. The Legends all agree that head movement is a killer; all golfers should strive to keep their heads motionless.
4. We need to be relaxed (think: stand at ease). Snead describes the position as "comfortably square."
5. Golfers should practice a relaxed stance until it becomes a habit.

8
Alignment

Take Dead Aim.
—Harvey Penick

Quite frankly, there is a lot of crap that gets handed out about what to do to play better golf. No one was better at sifting through all that than Harvey Penick. He got right to the point when he gave lessons. He wasn't interested in impressing students with what he knew about golf when he wanted to tell them what they needed to know in order to get better. I agree with Harvey. That is what teaching is all about. His advice on how to hit the ball straighter for some of his students was simple: "Take Dead Aim." Now he didn't just say those words and walk off, but his advice was really that simple. "Your body will do what your mind tells it to do. You have no doubt, no fear. For those few seconds you are what you think. That's Taking Dead Aim. Trust yourself."[81]

Too many times we get concerned about things that just don't matter, and Harvey had a way of reminding us that we should stop worrying about those things and focus on the task at hand. We should all quit worrying about how our swing looks and concentrate on the important thing at hand. In this case, where do we want the ball to go? Taking dead aim means more than just thinking about where we want the ball to go; it means getting the entire mind thinking that our chosen target is where the ball is going. Players with high handicaps will be surprised to find that if they focus on the task instead of worrying, they will get better results. Harvey advises, "[D]o it every time on every shot."[82] That is positive thinking at its very best.

That is not all I am going to say about alignment, but it is a good place to start. Arnold Palmer describes an "…imaginary target line, which runs from the ball straight to the target."[83] If we listen to any of the Legends, they all talk about an imaginary line that runs from the ball to the target. It might be surprising to know

Figure 8.1 Alignment

that they each have a specific target for each shot—not just an area on the fairway, but a specific target on that fairway, nor just the green, but a specific target on the green. Tom Watson hits his ball on long shots through imaginary goal posts whether he is bending the shot right or left.

Readers might be saying to themselves that they are not skilled enough to have a finite target, but their brains don't know that, and the brain needs a specific target. None of the folks who were at NASA in 1961 were satisfied to aim their first rocket simply into space and then hope it would land in the Caribbean. They had very minute calculations to ensure that their rocket went exactly where it was intended to go. The human brain needs specific targets to function at its best; it is smart enough to handle them. In golf, it all starts with proper alignment. The first step is described by Arnie. Golfers need to pick out the target for each particular shot. From the ball to the target runs an imaginary line. It is called the ball-target line. In figure 8.2, the target is the flag.

Figure 8.2 Ball-target line

The second step is for the golfer to pick out a spot or an object along that line to give him or her a reference point on that line three to five feet from the ball to help establish a parallel line of reference (see figure 8.2). This makes it easier to establish the alignment line. In this scenario, the leaf is that point of reference. At this point, we have identified three critical points—the specific target, the ball-target line, and the intermediary target. All three are critical in order to sustain proper alignment.

The next step is for the golfer to establish an alignment line (see figure 8.3). This is a line upon which the stance is based. It is a line running parallel to the ball-target line. The stance is adjusted according to the type of shot that is going to be hit. It is important to align the knees, hips, and shoulders with the ball-target line since we want to swing along the ball-target line. This produces a straight shot.

The sight line is the visual a golfer sees as he looks out at the target. Depending on the club he is hitting, he will be over the ball-target line with the putter looking directly at the target. With all the other clubs, the golfer will be inside the ball-target line and the distance

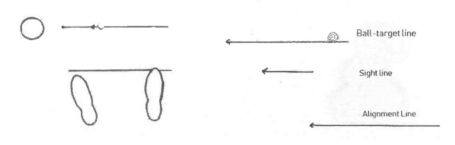

Figure 8.3 Alignment line

Figure 8.4 Sight line

will be the largest with the driver. With each of these clubs it will appear that the golfer is aimed to the left of the target. Look at the golfer on the railroad tracks (see figure 8.5) and imagine that he turns his head to the left so that he will be looking at the bushes to the left of the green, or aimed to the left of the target.

This could make him want to change his stance and aim more to the right. This happens to a lot of golfers. But we can tell that his aim is absolutely correct by the railroad tracks running directly to his target. This is why we establish a parallel alignment line to our ball-target line. It sets up an imaginary railroad track to the target. None of us should be fooled by convergence.

Convergence is the phenomenon of two points closing on each other in the distance and becoming one. What is thirty inches apart right in front of us closes to no gap in the distance. When we begin to align ourselves, we must remember to remain parallel to the ball-target line.

Figure 8.5 Convergence

Here is the problem. If I tell a student to line up parallel to the target line without any explanation, there is a very good chance that he will line up parallel and then look at the target and see that he is aimed way to the left. Our sight line does not converge like the railroad track in the drawing, and it never will. This visual image plays tricks on all unwary golfers. Golfers will adjust their stance according to their sight lines, not according to the ball-target line. When this happens, golfers will no longer be aligned on a line that runs parallel to the ball-target line. They are now aiming to the right of the target. The simple fact is that the parallel line (the alignment line) visually diverges from the target when we look up from it. It runs to the left side of the target, and it actually gets farther away (diverges) from the target the farther it extends. Until golfers get comfortable with this, they will feel like they are lined up way to the left of the target.

The dotted lines in figures 8.6, 8.7, and 8.8 indicate the ball-target line.

Figure 8.6 Square

Figure 8.7 Open

Figure 8.8 Closed

If the shoulders, hips, knees, and feet are squared up to both the ball-target line and the alignment line, the chances are very good that a golfer will swing his club along the ball-target line, and the clubhead will be square at impact producing a straight shot. Golfers must not be fooled by what they see in the distance.

If a golfer's shoulders, hips, and knees are open to both the ball-target line and alignment line, the chances are very good that he will swing the club from the outside the ball-target line, and the clubhead will be open at impact producing a shot that fades, slices, or is pulled to the left.

If the shoulders, hips, and knees are closed to both the ball-target line and the alignment line, the chances are very good that a golfer will swing the club from inside the ball-target line, and the clubhead will be closed at impact producing a shot that draws, hooks, or is pushed to the right of the target.

It is possible to check body alignment by using a club to align the knees, hips, and shoulders during practice sessions until the golfer is confident that he is aligning correctly. This may seem like a silly routine, but it does help orient the shoulders to the hips and the hips to the knees. They all must be aligned with the swing line to produce the desired shot.

Alignment drill. Like most of the other fundamentals we've discussed, alignment needs to be practiced and perfected. There are drills that work specifically to hone the skills necessary to form proper alignment. One of my favorites is a drill that only requires a golfer to have three golf clubs and a ball. The golfer should place the ball on the ground and move behind it. Next, he should pick out a target and an intermediate target. We will approach this ball as if it was in the fairway, but it should make no difference if it was on the tee; the approach is just the same.

1. The golfer should first determine the target.
2. Next, he should determine the ball-target line.
3. Picking out an intermediary target will enable the golfer to align himself more accurately.
4. Once the first three steps are established, the golfer should lay one of the golf clubs along the ball-target line.
5. He should then use the second club to establish the stance line by placing it on the ground parallel to the ball-target line.
6. Both of his feet should be lined up on the stance line in the golfer's preferred stance.
7. Finally, the golfer may use the third club to check the alignment of his knees, hips, and shoulders, making sure that they are all parallel to the stance line.

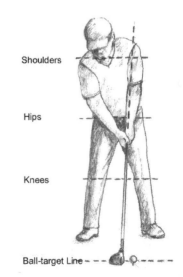

Figure 8.9 Parallel alignment

8. Golfers may repeat these steps, taking their preferred stance until the alignment can be checked without the aid of the golf clubs.

9. This drill should be done without the aid of the golf clubs on the ground to test the golfer's ability to automatically align himself properly.

Alignment Wrap-up

1. Taking dead aim means getting the entire mind and body focused on the target.

2. No golfer should ever aim at a general area; every golfer should have a specific target in mind each time he or she strikes the ball.

3. Golfers should pick out a spot on the target line about three to five feet in front of the ball and use this as a reference point to align the body parallel to the ball-target line.

4. We should never let divergence and convergence play tricks with where we are aiming.

9
Ball Position

Golf ball position requires consistency. For golfers who want to improve their games, hit the ball solidly, and score, they need to know where to set up the ball. I am guessing that the majority of golfers don't have a precise idea of where the ball goes for each of the clubs in the bag. We are going to correct that.

Figure 9.1 Bottom of the arc

We have certain fundamentals that are constants in the game of golf. The golf grip is a constant. It should not be the same for every club in the bag, with the possible exception of the putter. Our alignment procedure is a constant. We should establish the target, ball-target line, the intermediary target, and alignment line in the same manner on every hole. We have one golf swing, and it is consistent for every club in the bag, except the putter. We should not improvise on the swing.

2 Inches

The Legends have varying opinions about the best ball positions. Since individual body types make each swing arc unique, there is no one location that will work for every player. Some experimentation will be necessary. However, what is outlined here is a good place to start.

Figure 9.2 Placement of ball

First of all, creating a consistent swing will produce a consistent swing arc. This arc changes with the length of the club, and the location of the ball gets closer or farther from the golfer's body because the arc of the swing gets larger or smaller. The location relative to the instep does not change because the swing should be the same for every club.

The placement of the ball on an imaginary line extending from the instep of the front foot establishes swing consistency because the ball is at the bottom of the swing arc. If the golfer moves the ball back (one ball width) from this imaginary line to facilitate hitting on the downswing the arc of the swing does not change. The golfer must be sure to keep his head motionless and behind the ball. If the golfer moves the ball forward of this line (two ball widths) the swing arc again does not change; it only facilitates hitting on the upswing. The ball position has moved and the strike of the ball has changed from a sweep to a descending or ascending contact.

Figure 9.1 shows the bottom of the arc located off the instep of the left foot. The outside of the swing arc is the maximum distance that the clubhead will be located from the body at the bottom of the swing arc. It is easy to imagine that the arc of the wedge will be closer to the body than the arc of the driver due to the varying lengths of the different clubs. This is the reason that the ball position is not static. Therefore, the location of the ball moves in and out along the imaginary line from the instep to the outside arc of whichever club is being used. This is the ball position that Nicklaus played; he modified the position as shown in figure 9.2 by moving the ball position for his driver forward two ball widths. This was done to increase the loft and carry of his driver. The bottom of the swing arc is critical to identify because it prepares the golfer to correctly strike the ball for the three different shots required in the game.

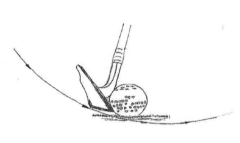

Figure 9.3 Descending strike

There are three possible contact points on the swing arc: descending, sweeping, and ascending. The descending point of contact between club and ball happens before the club reaches the bottom of the arc. This is often referred to as hitting down on the ball, a phrase that frequently causes golfers to change the action during their swings that almost always introduces errors. Saying that I am hitting down on the ball makes me think I am chopping wood or wielding a sledge hammer trying to pound something into the ground. It is important that we wipe this image from our minds. Instead, we should swing the club exactly like we do on every other shot. With the hands placed slightly in front of the ball, we should hit through the ball with no adjustment to our swing.

The shorter clubs have a shorter, thus steeper, arc; by swinging with a normal swing, that naturally steeper arc causes the ball to be struck first and then the ground, causing a divot. The wedges and higher lofted irons through the eight are played to be hit with a descending ball strike that takes a divot after contacting the ball. This produces backspin, accuracy, and holding power on the greens. Adjusting the position of the ball on the ball line extending from the left instep will allow the steeper swing arc to work.

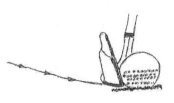

Figure 9.4 Sweeping strike

Sweeping, or hitting at the bottom of the arc, allows the club to graze the surface of the hitting area just after it makes contact with the ball. Golfers should adjust the ball position along the ball line to determine where the swing arc crosses the ball line. This swing is used for the midirons, hybrids, and the fairway woods, which are designed to be hit with a sweeping blow. The club path brushes the grass, but takes no divot, and produces moderate spin rates.

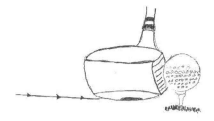

The ascending ball strike is used for the driver because the arc is greatest with the driver. The ascending ball strike happens after the club has passed the bottom of its swing arc and is on the rise. This ball strike increases the angle of attack of the driver and allows the golfer to put more loft on the ball, giving the ball more carry and lower rotation.

Figure 9.5 Ascending strike

Moving the ball forward for the driver, but still along the imaginary line extending from the left (or front) foot, keeps the head behind the ball, but will allow the swing arc to contact the ball on the ascending portion of the arc. The key to this placement is to hit through the ball and allow the ascending direction of the clubhead to do the work without having the clubhead touch the ground.

Ball Position Wrap-up

1. We have only one swing to use for striking the ball. To set up properly, we need to know where the bottom of the swing arc is for the club we are using.

2. The bottom of the swing arc moves closer to our feet as the clubs get shorter.

3. Descending, sweeping, and ascending are the three types of ball strikes we can make. We decide which strike to use by the club chosen and by the type of shot we are hitting.

4. The instep line is an imaginary, perpendicular line running from our left instep to the ball-target line. Nicklaus placed his ball on the instep line for each club except when using the driver; he then moved the ball forward for an ascending strike.

5. Other Legends moved the ball position relative to the instep line depending on the location of the bottom of their swing arc. When using the driver, some of the Legends placed the ball in front of the instep line. For midirons and fairway woods, some of the Legends placed the ball on the instep line, and with the short irons, the balls were sometimes placed in back of the instep line. Balls should not be placed behind the midline of a golfer's stance.

6. Once we determine the bottom of our swing arc, then we can establish the ball positions that work best.

10
The Footwork

Foot action is one of the main differences between a good golfer and a duffer.
—Sam Snead

"Footwork—The forgotten Fundamental"[84] is how Sam Snead describes footwork. The grip is a golfer's connection to his club, and footwork is his connection to the ground. Every professional athlete knows that he or she relies on footwork to arrive at the top of his or her respective sport. Every professional golfer has excellent footwork, but we rarely hear anyone talk about his or her footwork, which probably makes many golfers ask the obvious question: If footwork is so important, then why haven't we been hearing about this from our instructors or reading about it in golfing magazines or hearing the commentators on TV talking about it? Why is it a big dark secret?

Here is the explanation. No one ever told us how to walk; we learned it implicitly, and to learn anything implicitly means to learn something without lessons, without explicit instruction. That is how a young golfer learns footwork. Since most touring professionals and teaching professionals learned golf at a very young age, their footwork was part of the acquisition and progression of skills that came naturally, much like walking.

Remember when I tried to explain how I went from the middle lane to the right-hand lane? I had been performing the correct actions for so long that I no longer could explain correctly how and what I was doing. It has become a natural occurrence for me, and I no longer need to think about the physical motions involved; as far as I am concerned, it just happens. To golfers with a good golf swing, the footwork is so subtle that it goes almost unnoticed. They will focus for hours on the merits of swing tempo and release, but forget that without the movements of their feet—the weight being transferred from the front foot to the back foot and back to front again in balance—nothing good could have happened.

Nothing just happens in golf, and footwork makes a difference just like each specific action I perform while changing lanes driving seventy miles per hour on a highway makes a difference, but these actions are not so obvious when every action is done correctly, like the footwork we see in

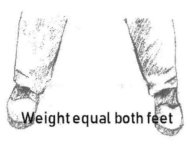

Figure 10.1 Balance

the world's top golfers. We only notice improper actions on the highway when we hit something, yet it seems that when obvious problems arise in our golf games, we don't think to analyze each distinct action involved in the footwork from the preshot routine all the way through the completion of our swing.

During the backswing, down pressure is increased on the instep of the back foot. The COM has moved to the right side of the core as the body rotates to facilitate the backswing. Good footwork keeps the body and the fluid motion of the swing in balance by focusing the down pressure on the instep of the back foot. To maintain balance and ensure an in-to-out-to-in swing path, the golfer increases the down pressure on the front foot prior to the beginning of the swing. It is part of the process that happens so naturally for those who know how to do it that talking about it never occurs to the commentators. In figure 10.1, the weight is distributed equally on both feet. The golfer is in balance.

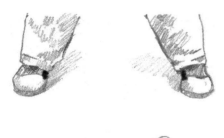

Figure 10.2 Balance on insteps

In the second drawing (figure 10.2), the golfer takes his stance to prepare to hit a golf ball with his driver. He bends his knees and applies down pressure equally to the insteps of both feet in preparation for the dynamic movement that is the golf swing. He does not root his feet into the ground as a football player would because this is not a contact sport. The movement he will support is not a lateral move, it is a rotary move, and he must be agile and in balance throughout the swing.

The first movement in the golf swing requires increasing the down pressure on the instep of the back foot (see figure 10.3). This move supports the one-piece rotary takeaway of the shoulders, arms, hands, and hips along with the supporting movement of the legs and feet. The instep down pressure on the right foot moves 60 to 80 percent of the weight to that side. We know that six out of the seven Legends raised the left heel to facilitate the rotation (figure 10.4).

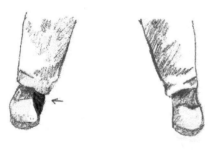

Figure 10.3 Down pressure to rear

When the weight is shifted, the golfer's COM moves to the right of the belt buckle, and that is why golfers need to keep their weight inside the insteps. When we practice, we must feel that our feet are involved until their involvement becomes second nature, a habit. The backswing is complete when the wrist cock is complete. Before the downswing starts and the swing changes direction, the down pressure is shifted to the front-foot instep (see figure 10.5). This is a critical move. It is to ensure that the downswing will follow an in-to-out swing path.

Figure 10.4 Raising the left heel

Figure 10.5 Down pressure to the front

Figure 10.6 Rotation to front

The front leg braces the left side as the golfer rotates through the swing. Pressure builds and this brace prevents him from moving ahead of the ball, allowing him to complete the rotary movement. After impact, as the golfer completes the release with his arms and hands, the down pressure will be transferred to the heel of the left foot (figure 10.6). At this point, 90 percent or more of the body weight will be on the front side.

Times are changing, but in the United States, our brains still don't talk to our feet. We are not a country that plays foot sports. We have pretty good hand-eye coordination, but our feet live in a different area code. So, we are a bit clumsy when it comes to getting them to do dance steps or any new action, but what follows is a simple drill that will improve our ability to hit golf balls. It's called the Squash Bugs Drill. It only requires a bit of imagination and a mirror.

Squash bugs drill. Down pressure change is key to the golf swing. The change in COM is accomplished, not by a shift of body weight but by muscle tension in the legs. The words *shift weight* cause many golfers to think of lateral movement, which often means they end up using their upper bodies to transfer weight. The golf swing is a rotary movement. The object of this drill is to help golfers learn to use down pressure instead of a shift or lateral movement to relocate the weight. What we want to do is move the down pressure from one foot to the other without moving the body. We must transfer the down pressure from the instep of the right foot in the backswing

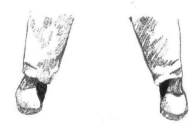

Figure 10.7 Balance on insteps

to the instep of the left foot prior to swinging the club on the downswing. Both moves are necessary to maintain balance and control.

Figure 10.7 shows the weight equally distributed on the insides of both feet. This should be the starting point for this drill.

1. Golfers should take a stance position looking in a mirror for this drill. It is important that all golfers make sure their weight is distributed equally on the insteps of both feet.

2. Without moving any part of the upper body, the golfer should increase the down pressure on the right foot. This is easy if golfers can imagine that they are squashing bugs under the instep of that foot. To do this properly, it is important to focus on using the muscles on the inside of the right leg. Golfers should now feel pressure on the instep of the right foot, and the left foot should feel lighter. This is exactly what happens in the first move of the takeaway. Weight is transferred to the instep of the back foot. We accomplish this through down pressure and not through a lateral shift.

3. Golfers should continue looking in the mirror while they change the down pressure from the right foot to the left foot. It should be done with no movement in the upper body.

4. To accomplish this, golfers need to focus on the muscles in the inside of the left leg and relax the right leg.

5. It is important for us to practice this movement of down pressure until we are able to move the pressure (weight) from one side of the body to the other with no discernable movement in the upper body.

Advanced squash bugs drill. Once golfers can shift their weight from one foot to the other without any discernable movement in the upper body, they are ready for a challenge.

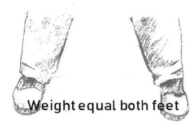

Figure 10.1 Balance

1. Those ready for the advanced version of this drill should start with step one above, establishing a stance position while looking in the mirror to make sure the body's weight is evenly distributed between both feet (see figure 10.1).

2. During step two of this drill, however, golfers can add the rotation of the hips and shoulders away from what would be the target while simultaneously increasing the down pressure on the right (back) foot (see figure 10.3). Golfers should keep their hands on their hips while doing this drill. This should be repeated until the weight can shift to the instep of the right foot with no lateral movement visible during the upper-body rotation.

3. In step three, first the hips and then the shoulders should rotate toward what would be the target while simultaneously increasing the down pressure back onto the left (front) foot (see figure 10.5). Repeat this until the weight can be established on the instep of the left foot with no visible lateral movement in the rotation of the upper body.

4. To be most effective, this drill should be practiced in front of a mirror.

5. Golfers should practice every day for two weeks, and the down-pressure drill will become fixed in the motor cortex. After that, golfers will only occasionally have to think about down pressure or weight transfer.

Footwork Wrap-up

1. Our footwork is our connection to the ground and controls where our center of mass (COM) will be.
2. Our COM determines the direction and bottom of the swing arc.
3. Ideally, we want our COM to be perpendicular to the ball strike zone.
4. We set up with the weight evenly distributed on the insteps of both feet. We are in balance, and our COM is in the center of our bodies.
5. As the backswing is initiated, the down pressure moves to the instep of the right foot, and the COM moves to right side of the body.
6. Before the downswing begins, down pressure is transferred to the instep of the left foot. COM is now opposite the ball, allowing for the swing arc to be inside-to-inside. Golfers should not push off with the back foot.
7. After the ball strike, the weight moves to the heel of the left foot, which allows the rotation to complete itself in the follow-through.
8. Our feet must remain active. They are not rooted in the ground. In order to achieve this active footwork, the lower body must remain active as well during the golf swing.

11
Rotation

You will never hit the ball consistently long and straight if you slide or sway your hips significantly toward the target on the downswing.
—Jack Nicklaus

Golf is a rotary sport. We swing around our bodies, not down a line in front of our bodies (figure 11.1). Most golfers think the backswing is the beginning of the hitting action, but, for the experienced golfer, it is not the beginning of the action. I have written earlier that the Legends all say that golf is not a static sport. The reason they say that is because it is difficult to start any dynamic move from a dead stop.

Figure 11.1 Backswing rotation

The preshot routine can and should be a movement action itself. If golfers learn a proper preshot routine, they are already in motion—they are light on their feet, they are not locked to the ground, and the last move the experienced golfer makes prior to the backswing is the forward press.

Harvey Penick had an image he liked to talk about: "swing the bucket."[85] To do this, he pictured himself holding a bucket full of water. If he holds it on the sides and tries to swing it, he would have to start by rocking it forward a bit before it could swing to the rear. This rocking action would begin the rotation to the rear. Penick further explained that if he were gripping the bucket tightly, his rotation would be fast, and if he were gripping the bucket lightly, the turn would be light and free. This was his explanation of how golfers should approach the forward press.

Using a forward press was a useful tool in the Legends' arsenals, and it is another habit we all need to form. It is like placing our hands on the table prior to getting up from a meal or from our desks at work. We can think of seeing a basketball player dribble the ball three times and spinning it in his hands prior to taking his free throw or the gymnast who takes two deep breaths before she begins her tumbling routine.

There is nothing old fashioned or artificial about a good forward press. "It helps keep a young swing fluid and an old swing young."[86] The types of forward presses differ, but they all serve the same purpose. They keep the golfer moving. Jones relied on the "little forward twist of the hips,"[87] which was his rotation of the hips counterclockwise to effectively start his swing. Nicklaus used the forward press of the club, and Snead pressed the club and the knee forward to get things started. All these moves were designed to create movement to allow the rotary action of the swing to be a reactive movement rather than a beginning from a cold start.

Figure 11.2 identifies the parts of the one-piece takeaway: the shoulders, the arms, and the hands. All three of these parts act as a unit. They rotate together to the rear and are controlled by the large muscles of the shoulders and back. The small muscles of the hands are not as reliable in controlling this first move. The core of the body brings the hips into the rotational action. Jones wrote, "It is very plain that the hands and club are started back by the rotation of the player's trunk and the movement of the arms."[88] Palmer, Nicklaus, and Hogan write that the desired one-piece takeaway movement is controlled by the rotation of the shoulders so that the initial movement is controlled by the large muscles of the back and shoulders (figure 11.3).

As the club moves above waist high, the arms and wrists become involved as the wrist cock and the lifting action become part of the backswing. We get the club waist high through rotation of the shoulders and hips only. As the clubhead moves up over the shoulder, it is directed toward the slot. At the top of the backswing, the rotation is complete, and the club finds the slot (figure 11.4). The separation between the rotation of the shoulders and the rotation of the hips is between thirty-five and forty-five degrees. Ideally, we would like the shoulders to rotate ninety degrees and the hips to rotate forty-five degrees. Just as the club reaches the top of the swing the transition begins (figure

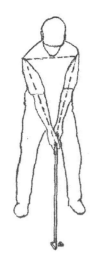

Figure 11.2 The triangle

Figure 11.3 Rotation of the trunk

Figure 11.4 Finding the slot

11.5). Down pressure is shifted to the front instep in preparation for the downswing.

While performing the backswing, especially when paying attention to the rotation that drives the motion, golfers should remember that the down pressure remains on the instep of the right foot (back foot), and this back foot should be planted at a ninety-degree angle to prevent overrotation of the hips and, at the same time, create torque in the back and the abdominals, which promotes speed in the downswing. It is important to keep the club in front of the chest as the body rotates and the club moves backward from its starting position. Ideally, the shoulders should rotate ninety degrees, and the hips should follow at forty-five degrees.

Figure 11.5 Transition

The takeaway and backswing rotation should be completed at the topmost point of the swing; this is the transition point. The cocking of the wrists should also be completed at this point in the swing. This is the point at which the rotation changes direction. The down pressure shifts from the right foot (or back foot) to the instep of the lead foot, which is the left foot for most golfers, allowing the rotation to begin from the ground up; legs and hips lead with the torso, shoulders, and arms following. All rotation should be completed when both the shoulders and the belt buckle are aimed at the target.

Rotation Wrap-up

1. Golf is a rotary sport. Nothing good is achieved by sliding toward the target. The hips don't slide; they rotate.
2. During the backswing, the shoulders, the arms, and the hands act as a unit as they rotate to the rear, guided by the large muscles of the back.
3. In the downswing, down pressure is transferred to the left foot, and the hips start to uncurl and rotate toward the target.
4. The shoulders follow in a rotary motion, bringing the arms along with them.
5. The rotation of the body is completed as the chest ends up facing the target.

Part IV

12
The Takeaway

The first part of the golf swing, the start or takeaway, must be done correctly every time. The end product—proper contact with the ball—is in jeopardy once the club starts moving. In that way, it is like the start of a one-hundred-meter race. Since 1896, the Olympic one-hundred-meter dash has seen times dropping throughout the years as start technique has played a bigger role in training. The current record is 9.63 seconds and is held by a man named Usain Bolt. His starts are explosive; he needed only four perfect starts to achieve the gold medal. Golf is like that but on a larger scale—in both sports the perfect start is the key.

For example, to win the coveted green jacket at the Masters, the champion needs about 144 perfect starts, or takeaways, to avoid disaster. Jack Nicklaus states, "In fact, the longest slump in my career was caused by an incorrect takeaway movement that became habitual and thus very difficult to cure."[89] Everything in golf is said to be counterintuitive, and that axiom applies to the takeaway. The brain wants to speed up when the secret is to slow down.

Beginning the backswing is like driving slowly through a school zone when in a hurry. The driver must remember to slow down every time. "The first two feet establish your tempo and swing path."[90] The initial path must be correct and done at the right speed in order to produce a repeatable swing. We help ourselves to do this by taking the club away in a move called the one-piece takeaway (see figure 12.1). "Your left shoulder, arm, and hand start the backswing in unison."[91] The triangle formed by the shoulders, arms, and hands moves the clubhead away from the ball. The straight left arm guarantees the swing arc will be at its maximum. Initiating the movement with the shoulders keeps the hands out of the action and allows us to use the big muscles in the back, which are more suited for controlled movement under pressure. The hands remain steady and do not move at all until the club reaches a point, waist high,

One piece takeaway

Figure 12.1 One-piece takeaway

Figure 12.2 Extend to rear

back along a line parallel to the target line and horizontal to the ground (figure 12.2). At this point—because of the rotation of the hips, shoulders, and torso—the toe of the club points straight up, and the cocking movement begins. Golfers must keep in mind that the entire swing takes less than one and a half seconds, and the majority of that time is during the backswing.

The triangle created by the arms, shoulders, and hands is not intended to be rigid, so golfers should relax. No one can swing a golf club if he or she is tense. We must think of keeping the triangle firm and in front of our chest as we rotate away from the target. The hands should remain firm until the rotation of the shoulders and hips have brought the club to horizontal; only then should the wrists begin the cock.

Golfers should always think about moving slowly in the takeaway. Penick advises us that "A slow backswing gives you time to make a good turn and stay balanced as you are gathering yourself for the forward blow."[92]

Tempo is a factor that is often discussed, but rarely taught. It is the rate at which the club is swung back and then down through the ball. It is often regulated by the temperament of the individual and, more specifically, by how the individual feels on any given day. However, the backswing should be consistent and always go back slowly, and then, after the transition, the downswing should increase in speed as it comes down to the contact point. Even though the entire swing can take less than one and a half seconds, there are variations of swing tempos between golfers—some swing tempos are faster, some are slower. When we practice, we should pay attention to each shot and consciously try to slow down and find a tempo that works. Then that tempo should be used for each swing. Nicklaus suggests improving the tempo by taking time on the practice tee to swing the club, "timing your foot motion to the dance tempo…one-two-three, one-two-three…."[93] Consistency pays dividends, so golfers need to learn what playing rhythm works for them and stick with it.

The feet will remain in the same location where they started, but they are active throughout the swing. The left heel may rise in the backswing and be replanted in the downswing. As the shoulders rotate away from the target, simultaneously weight is transferred to the instep of the rear foot through down pressure. This is not a lateral movement (see the Squash Bugs Drill at the end of chapter 10). The golfer increases the down pressure on the rear foot and keeps his weight inside his body's framework to secure his balance.

We should think of the backswing as winding up, creating torque so that we can use the stored torque coming down to deliver speed to the ball strike. The goal is to achieve a ninety-degree rotation with the shoulders and about half that with the hips. This rotation is stored energy.

The takeaway is done with the left arm straight, but not stiff, and the direction is initially straight down the ball-target line. Golfers should let the rotation of their hips, torso, the triangle (made by the arms, shoulders, and hands), and the club length dictate how long the club follows the ball-target line. The goal is to create as big an arc as possible. The shoulder turn and a straight left arm will establish the proper arc in the takeaway.

When golfers swing the club back from the ball with the one-piece takeaway, the club should travel along the ball-target line and move inside without help from the golfer. Golfers should not try to manipulate this by altering the takeaway and forcing the club inside with the hands. The arc of a golfer's swing depends on how much deviation there is from the ball-target line.

Golfers should be sure that their hands are in the same place each time they start their take-away. If the hands start from a different place, then the takeaway will not have the desired consis-tency. The Legends recommend that the hands be positioned just in front of the front leg's inside thigh. Bobby Jones had this to say about movement of the hands: "The actual fact is that in the correct golf swing there is very little pronation of the left hand or rotation of the left forearm during the backswing, and the effort to introduce either is about as harmful as anything a player can do."[94] Simply stated, anything that a golfer does with his hands in the takeaway or backswing to manipulate the face of the club is wrong. Golfers should keep their hands still.

Rotation, or rolling, the wrists during the backswing is a common fault of middle- and high-handicap golfers. There should be no rolling of the wrists; this is called either supination or pronation depending on the direction of the rotation. If a golfer supinates or pronates during the backswing, she must then add the reverse motions to correct for those moves when she begins to uncock the wrists and is coming down at a much faster rate. This complicates the swing. It is important to keep the wrists quiet. The right hand will pronate and the left hand will supinate during the release, but this doesn't happen until the club contacts the ball.

There should be no cupping of the wrists; this is called either wrist flexion or extension depending on whether the movement is pushing the palm of the hand or the back of the hand toward the arm. Some golfers do this as they hit the ball thinking that wrist action will aid in getting the ball airborne. However, that is what the clubface is designed to do, so golfers should let it work for them.

The only wrist action in the backswing will be cocking. Cocking action is a side-to-side action moving the thumbs toward the forearms. To understand the wrist cock, a golfer can take his grip and hold the club in front of him. He then moves his thumbs toward his chest. This is the wrist cock. This action starts when he reaches the halfway point or, more specifically, when the club is parallel to the ground and the clubhead gets higher than the hands. The larger the wrist-cock angle just prior to the downswing, the greater the swing velocity.

Golfers should keep the head motionless and behind the ball throughout the entire swing. Head movement side to side and up and down, even slight movements, can cause golfers to mishit the golf ball, so if mishits occur, golfers should focus on keeping the head motionless. A few professionals move the head away from the target in the backswing, but it moves only slightly and remains motionless when the downswing begins.

Takeaway drill. This is a simple drill to work on the one-piece takeaway. It is important to use the muscles in the shoulders and back, not the hands.

Figure 12.3 Step drill

1. To initiate the takeaway, all golfers should rotate the shoulders and then the hips and change the down pressure to the right (back) foot.
2. The club should move straight back slowly until it is at waist height as seen in figure 12.3. Moving the club straight back to start will create the best chance for straight-through movement at the finish of the swing.
3. When the horizontal point is reached, the clubhead will be pointing straight up if positioned correctly. The shoulders will have rotated ninety degrees to the rear.
4. The golfer should then pivot on his right foot and step around onto his left and return the club to the ground. The golfer should finish in his setup stance.
5. It is important to check the clubface to see that it is square with the new ball-target line.
6. If the triangle has been maintained, the hands have not been used in the takeaway, and the shoulders and hips have rotated properly, the golfer should be aligned to repeat the drill, rotating around in a circle. He should return to the original starting point with four repetitions of the drill.
7. The entire torso and the feet are involved in the takeaway, but it is important to stay relaxed and loose while using each of the parts involved. If the takeaway becomes a hands and arm movement only, big trouble awaits. By practicing the one-piece takeaway regularly, golfers will soon reap the benefits.

Takeaway Wrap-up

1. The takeaway is initiated by increase in down pressure on the right instep.

2. The club is moved slowly along the ball-target line with shoulder rotation in control. The hip rotation follows the shoulders, joined by the arms and hands. This movement controls the swing of the club until it reaches waist height.

3. During the takeaway, the backswing, and the transition, the hands hold the club and do not rotate (neither supinating nor pronating), nor do they cup, which is either flexing or extending.

4. The function of the hands and wrists is to cock as the clubhead passes through waist height.

13
The Backswing

Figure 13.1 Backswing

The initial setup to the ball determines whether a golfer has an upright swing stance as in figure 13.2 or a flat swing stance as in figure 13.3. There is no right or wrong stance. The setup and the stance are related to body type and individual preferences. As the shoulders and arms rotate, they create a swing plane that can be upright or flat. The key is that the swing extend back straight from the ball in a one-piece take-away. With a one-piece takeaway, golfers will be in control of the club when it moves up over the right shoulder with the upright swing or slightly across the back with the flat swing. The key is to end up with the club pointing toward the target.

Figure 13.2 Upright stance

There are pros and cons to both the upright swing and the flat swing. The first consideration relates to control. The upright swing plane remains in the hitting zone for a fraction longer than the flat swing plane because of the position of its arc, which is steeper. Many golfers argue that this gives the golfer more control. The flat swing is in the hitting

Figure 13.3 Flat stance

Figure 13.4 The triangle

Figure 13.5 Backswing wrist cock

zone for slightly less time with its flatter swing plane, which may cause a golfer to have slightly less control. The next issue relates to mastery. An upright swing is more difficult to master because the rotational movement of hips and torso are not in the same plane as the shoulder rotation. With the flatter swing, the rotation of the hips, torso, and shoulders are all in the same plane, making it easier to learn. The flatter arc is considered to be more powerful, so, for the average golfer, it will impart more swing speed. Regardless of which swing a golfer uses, the backswing basics remain the same for all golfers.

First, no matter which swing is used, the golfer must stay behind the ball throughout the swing sequence, and it is important for the golfer to keep his head motionless and maintain the shoulder-arm-hand triangle for as long as possible (figure 13.4).

Figure 13.6 Going to the slot

Figure 13.7 Top of the swing, the slot

Second, we must remember that the backswing blends its beginning with the end of the takeaway as the club approaches horizontal. The club is raised up from horizontal and over, but not behind, the shoulder. This action moves the head of the club behind the head, and the extension of the left arm and folding of the right arm extend the reach of the club until it points toward the target. This is called the slot.

Once the head of the club passes the horizontal mark, the cocking action begins and the right arm begins to fold and acts as a stabilizer (figure 13.6). It also functions to guide and lift the club into the slot at the top of the swing. The left arm plays the key role throughout the backswing and the downswing. The Legends agree that the left arm should guide the swing arc. Rather than keep the left arm stiff as a board, it should be as straight as possible. An extended left arm establishes the largest possible arc for the swing. The slot is the topmost position of the backswing, but that position can be in a different place on the arc for every club.

Third, since the downswing begins from the slot, this position must be repeated on every swing at the end of the backswing: shoulder turn is ninety degrees, and hip turn is approximately forty-five degrees (figure 13.7). Starting from the slot each time builds downswing consistency. Overreaching on the backswing forces the golfer out of the slot and can cause the need to regrip, both of which create serious control problems.

The Backswing Wrap-up

1. During the backswing, the right arm folds and the left arm remains straight as the wrist is cocked and the club is raised up and over the shoulders to its position in the slot.
2. The slot is a position over the shoulders (not the back) and achieved by keeping the hands firm and only cocking the wrists. Once in the slot, the toe of the club points toward the target. Golfers should never lay the club off. Laying the club off happens when the wrist and forearm roll to the rear and out of the slot, allowing the shaft to angle across the back instead of in line with the shoulders. This means the golfer either has to realign the club at the bottom of the swing prior to making contact with the ball or the golfer will end up hitting the ball way off the target.
3. The upright and flat swings are both taken to the slot.

14
The Transition

A transition is described as the passage from one state to another; in this case, swinging back or up changes to swinging down or forward. This seems simple enough, but there is a lot riding on how well a golfer understands what should and what should not happen during the transition.

If we watch the very best golfers swing, the transition is almost imperceptible. The club merely changes direction and, as if by magic, goes in the opposite direction, increases speed, and contacts that one-and-a-half-inch object lying on the ground or tee. This change in direction will happen in less than three-tenths of a second. Palmer describes it as follows: "Whatever your natural body turn is, think of your hands as coasting to a stop at the top and as smoothly changing directions before picking up speed."[95]

Palmer's explanation makes it sound as easy as changing one's mind, but changing momentum and direction are more than that. To succeed, a golfer's transition will have to become an automatic phase of the swing. There is no time to think during the transition. The successful transition happens when a golfer has practiced the correct skills often enough to have saved the skill in the motor cortex of his brain, giving him the ability to perform the skill without having to signal each step from the brain to the body one by one. All successful golfers have developed this ability, and anyone who wants to become a better golfer can too. No golfer has the time to say to himself, "Okay, now change direction" and think of each step that must happen. We must practice until it becomes automatic. It just has to flow. So, what could go wrong?

This change of direction is started by the simultaneous rotation of the hips toward the target and the movement of down pressure from the inside of the right foot to the inside of the left foot. This is not a shift or a slide; it is a movement done with down pressure.

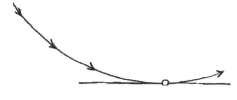

We want the club to reverse direction and follow, as nearly as possible, the same path it took on the way to the top. We want to have a swing path that comes from inside the ball-target line, travels down the ball-target line to make contact with the ball, and returns to the inside without crossing over the ball-target line (figure 14.1).

Figure 14.1 Inside-to-inside swing path

Figure 14.2 Out-to-in swing path

The club must travel straight down the ball-target line in order not to impart side spin on the ball. If our swing comes from the inside but, instead of traveling down the ball-target line, it crosses over the ball-target line before it reaches the ball, it will follow the swing arc back to the ball-target line and cross it from the outside as it strikes the ball (figure 14.2). This will impart side spin on the ball creating a slice or a pull. Swinging from the inside and along the ball-target line would be easy if we were a post with a pendulum suspended from the top (see figure 14.3). But we have two arms, not one, and two legs and two feet on the ground, not a single pole to swing around. The problem is to figure out how we can create a situation where we will be most like the post and the pendulum.

We could make sure our stance has equal amounts of weight on both feet and hold the club with both arms straightened and active with the same tension in both hands. With this weight distribution, the center of mass (COM) would be in the middle of our chest. If we swing from

Figure 14.3 Post and pendulum

this position, the bottom of the swing arc would be in the middle of our stance opposite the COM. Unfortunately, this stance would create an inefficient arm swing; that solution just doesn't work if our goal is to maximize the power and accuracy of our swing.

The better answer to more clubhead speed is to rotate our shoulders, torso, and hips. To accomplish this, one arm must be the pendulum and the other arm will have to act as a stabilizer. To create the pole and pendulum with our bodies, we have to swing with the majority of our weight on one leg, which becomes the pole, and allow the arm on that side to be the pendulum. We have to develop a method that allows us to rotate around that pole.

Figure 14.4 Top of the backswing

We set up with equal weight on both insteps in our golf stance to achieve balance. As we rotate the club away from the target, we use down pressure to transfer weight to the instep of our back foot and move the club to the top of the backswing (see figure 14.4). In the downswing, we transfer the down pressure to the front foot instep to hit the ball and unwind. Before the energy of the windup can be released, however, the golfer must establish a fixed post to rotate around to imitate the post and pendulum. The rotational movement of the legs, hips, torso, and shoulders are the driving forces of the golf swing, and this energy must be controlled by one post from the start of the swing. That post is on the front side.

This works, but we have trouble with controlling the direction of the ball flight when the club strikes. It spins when hit a glancing blow. The transfer of down pressure from the back foot to the front foot involves movement of the COM and a change in the apex of the swing arc. The COM establishes the apex of the swing arc. This COM is established by the down pressure on the left foot. This is critical to contacting the ball correctly.

If the golfer has not transferred his weight to his front side at the time the hip rotation begins, he is swinging with two posts (each leg being one) and this keeps the apex of the club arc back in the stance. With the ball placed off the instep of the front foot, this can produce an out-to-in swing path through the hitting zone. Without the transfer of down pressure to the front side when the hips start to move, the golfer will never swing through the hitting zone from the inside with accuracy and consistency.

As we look at the golf swing, it is really two arms blended into a one-arm swing. The left arm creates the swing arc through to contact, and it is joined briefly just after contact by the right arm. At this point, both arms are straight together as the release happens. The right arm and hand take over to finish the swing and release while the remainder of the body and the left arm provide stability and complete the rotation. To ensure that the left side (post) is fixed and is the point around which the swing will rotate, the down pressure must be transferred to the left foot simultaneously with the beginning of the hip rotation. The left shoulder becomes the ball joint (or top of the post) from which the arm swings, and the front hip becomes the axis on which the post (side) rotates.

In 2009, I asked a physicist to look at this problem, and she gave me what is now called Laura's Law.

> **Laura's Law**: Eighty percent of the weight must be transferred to the lead foot prior to beginning the golf swing to effectively establish the post-pendulum relationship necessary to avoid the out-to-in swing path. Degrees off center = arc tan(x in/66 in)*57 deg/rad, where the pendulum arc = arm and club, and x = length in inches between the person's belly button and the front leg.[96]

Laura's Law was formulated for a pendulum arc of sixty-six inches, which is the length of the driver and left arm combined, and with its center point (apex) opposite the left hip. In this calculation, the left side of the golfer became the post. When we set up, the apex of the arc is in the middle of our body opposite our COM. This is because the weight is evenly distributed on the insides of both feet (figure 14.5). A swing with this weight distribution will produce an out-to-in swing.

The apex of the swing arc moves opposite the rear hip (away from the post side) when we increase down pressure to the back foot (figure 14.6). Swinging with weight distribution predominately on the back foot will result in an out-to-in swing path.

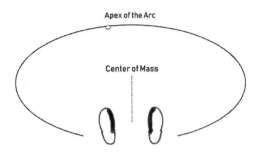

Figure 14.5 Weight centered

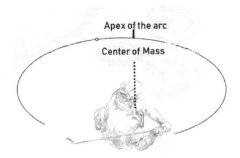

Figure 14.6 Back foot COM

The formula was developed to determine how far outside the ball-target line the clubhead would theoretically go if the weight was not shifted to the front foot prior to beginning the golf swing. For example, if x equals five inches and the center of mass, which establishes the apex of the swing arc, does not move to the left hip by transfer of the down pressure, the apex of the swing arc will remain opposite the right hip and an 8.3-degree, out-to-in swing is possible. If COM has moved to the belly button, the result is a 4.15-degree, out-to-in swing at the contact point. Both swings produce a slice or pull.

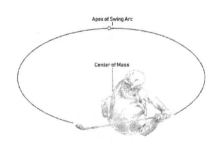

Figure 14.7 Front foot COM

In figure 14.7, the down pressure has transferred to the front side of the body and the COM has moved to the front side. The apex of the swing arc coincides with the placement of the ball opposite the instep of the left foot. This does not happen unless down pressure is transferred as the hip rotation begins. The downswing does not begin until the shoulders follow the hips and start to unwind.

The sequence is as follows: the down pressure is transferred to the front foot; almost simultaneously the hips begin their rotation to the front. With the down pressure on the front foot and the hip rotation in process, the counterclockwise shoulder turn begins. This action initiates the downswing of the arms. This order of the sequence is critical; there is no opportunity for adjustment once it begins.

We should think of golf as a speed game and not a power game. This is a problem that plagues athletes from other sports who like to dig in for extra power, which results in lateral movement. This is not something that will enhance a golf game. The lateral movement results from pushing off with the back foot. We must understand that this leaves the down pressure (weight) on the rear foot and the center of mass remains above the rear foot as the swing begins. There is no way to recover from here.

◁◁●▷▷

The Transition Wrap-up

1. At the top of the backswing arc is the slot. This slot is the starting point of the downswing. Golfers must swing the club to the slot position to have a repeatable downswing. Each golfer's slot position is unique just as each golfer's swing is unique.

2. During the transition, down pressure increases on the front (left) foot to give golfers a post around which to swing. This happens before the club has fully finished its backswing arc. Some Legends, like Sam Snead, talk of having an actual pause at the top of the swing, but to the casual observer, that pause is imperceptible.

3. This down pressure onto the left foot is the signal for the hips to begin the rotation back toward the front. The rotation is around the post created by the left foot, not through that side of the body. There should be no sliding action.

4. The club and shot dictate the length of the backswing. Consistency is achieved by the hands following the same backswing arc to the top of the swing. This means location of the slot (top of the backswing) can vary for each club, but the hands are on the same arc.

15
The Downswing

Figure 15.1 Downswing

The table has been set; we have moved through the takeaway, the backswing, and the transition, and we are just hundredths of a second from impacting the golf ball. We want our swing to follow a path as close as possible to the one that it took to the top of the backswing. This will ensure that it is on a swing path inside and then along the ball-target line. The clubhead will square up on the ball-target line and impact the ball with a blow that will direct it straight toward the target.

We set this in motion by proper timing of the increase of the down pressure onto our front foot during the transition. This gives us a post (or a side) to swing around. Sometimes terms are

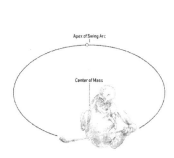

Figure 15.2 Inside-to-inside

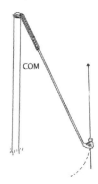

Figure 15.3 The post

confusing, and some instructions give us swing thoughts that are incorrect. Advice to swing from the inside and hit from inside the ball-target line is sometimes given to keep us from swinging the club outside the ball-target line. Swinging outside occurs when the club crosses the ball-target line. When golfers swing across the ball-target line and hit the ball, they put side spin on the ball, and it slices. In another scenario, golfers may be advised to close their clubface to guard against putting that spin on the ball, and they end up pulling the ball to the left. Both are wrong.

Thinking that we should hit from the inside is wrong too. What? Heresy! No, in the takeaway, our golf clubhead moves back on a straight line away from the ball and then moves inside the ball-target line with the rotation of our hips and shoulders. To hit the ball straight, the downswing must follow the same path in reverse. This means the swing should be straight down along the ball-target line just before impact. No golfer should force his swing to be inside the ball-target line. Instead, all golfers should let their swings unwind and swing down along the ball-target line.

Before beginning the downswing, the weight is still on the back foot (figure 15.4). We increase the torsion created in the backswing by transferring the down pressure from the instep of the back foot to the instep of the front foot and simultaneously rotating the hips toward the target. The change of down pressure is key to the transition and allows us to reverse the momentum of the backswing and set the club on a path back along the same arc. When the club reaches the top of the backswing, the wrist cock is complete, and the clock has been wound; now, with the weight on the front foot, we can let it unwind.

The rotation to the front has already begun. It started in the transition just before we completed the backswing. The rotation begins from the ground and travels up the legs through the hips. The shoulders follow this rotation and pull the arms along with them. The clubhead speed builds as it follows the backswing arc toward the contact zone. The entire downswing direction is controlled by the left arm as it is pulled by the unwinding of the hips, torso, and shoulders.

Figure 15.4 shows that the wrists remain cocked and the shoulders delay turning to the front while the hips rotate toward the front, creating more torque. The hands and wrists are in the same position they were in at the top of the swing when the cocking of the wrists was complete. In effect, the arms are pulled from the top by the rotation of the hips. We do not swing from the top with our arms or our hands.

The cocking of the wrists has set up what is described as a double pendulum. The double pendulum is so named because two pendulums join together on the downswing arc. The proper mating of these two pendulums increases the clubhead speed. Leg action, hip turn, and shoulder turn have combined to bring the body to this position. Proper uncocking of the wrists creates a second pendulum, and this pendulum joins the large pendulum on the same arc increasing the speed of the clubhead as it enters the hitting zone.

Figure 15.4 Unwinding the downswing

The Double Pendulum

We create the swing pendulum by the extension of the left arm and the golf club and the rotation of our hips, torso, and shoulders. The swing pendulum is the dominant factor in the golf swing we are all familiar with.

A second pendulum is created by uncocking our wrists (see figure 15.5). This wrist-cock pendulum must match the direction of the swing pendulum. If we pick up the club and cock the wrists, we find that the wrist-cock pendulum that is created is perpendicular to the ball-target line. If we rotate our shoulders ninety degrees away from the swing direction, we find that this second pendulum now lines up with the direction of the swing pendulum.

To understand this relationship, we need to take our stance and cock our wrists, seeing that the club goes away from us. If we turn our shoulders to the right, we see that the wrist-cock pendulum joins the arc of the swing pendulum when the shoulders are rotated to the rear. In the downswing, the uncocking of the wrists must occur while the shoulders are turned to the rear. This is where the two pendulums can match swing direction.

If the uncocking happens as the shoulders return parallel to the ball-target line, the clubhead will not stay on the intended line of the primary pendulum. The late uncocking movement moves the arc of the swing to a path that crosses the ball-target line from outside, creating an out-to-in path. This can cause a slice or a pull.

When the wrist-cock pendulum joins the swing pendulum, it can be a speed enhancer. This only happens when the uncocking action lags or is delayed until the pull of the clubhead has sufficiently built. This happens as the clubhead reaches the bottom third of the swing arc. At this point, the uncocking of the wrists happens and the two pendulums join. The combination of the wrist-cock pendulum with the swing pendulum boosts the clubhead speed just prior to impact. If the club is uncocked too soon, high in the swing arc, it is like a booster rocket that fails.

Figure 15.5 Double pendulum

Figure 15.6 Uncocking to impact

Uncocking into the Release

We have discussed the dominance of the straight left arm in controlling the takeaway through the transition and the backswing. The left arm remains the primary control over the golf swing from the beginning of the downswing and right through the point that the club passes horizontal. This dominance ensures that we bring the club back to the hitting zone on the same arc and path which it followed in getting to the top of the backswing.

As the club passes horizontal and reaches the bottom of the arc, the uncocking of the wrists happens, and we hit the ball hard with both hands. Hogan states clearly that "On a full shot you want to hit the ball as hard as you can with your right hand." He continues on to make the point that to achieve maximum power we need to, "Hit the ball as hard as you can with both hands."[97] If we let the left hand relax, we lose control and power. It is also likely that the right hand will overpower the left, and errors will occur. Figure 15.6 shows that the uncocking is nearly finished. The uncocking is complete just as the club makes contact with the ball, and the release has been initiated.

Figure 15.7 Right Hand Square   Figure 15.8 Right Hand begins   Figure 15.9 Right Hand in Full
Pronation   Pronation

As the uncocking is completed, the right hand and left hand both hit the ball, and hit it hard. The left hand and arm lead the strike into the ball, and the right arm and hand join in and take over as the ball is struck. The right arm is still slightly bent as the strike occurs, and the right arm and hand lead the follow-through by initiating the release just before or right at impact. Figure 15.7 shows the right hand at contact; it is square to the ball-target line. In the release, the right wrist and hand will turn or pronate. This pronation is visible in figure 15.8, showing the right hand after contact and the release in progress. The clubhead is being extended toward the target with the right arm fully extended and the left arm bending into the side. The release is complete upon full pronation of the right hand as seen in figure 15.9. When the club reaches horizontal, the palm of the right hand faces the ground. All four knuckles of the right hand are visible.

We must think of the release as the final move in the uncocking action. Up to this point, we have maintained our grip on the club with no movement of hands and wrists except to cock the club. As we uncock the club, it returns to the hitting zone square to the ball-target line where both hands hit the ball hard. After that comes the release.

Figure 15.10 The release

Figure 15.11 Follow-thru to finish

Figure 15.10 shows the release with the right arm fully extended toward the target. This extension maintains our swing arc, giving us maximum benefit from the size of the arc. The down pressure on the left side has moved all our weight to the front foot, and we complete our rotation with a high finish as shown in figure 15.11 above. The down pressure on the front foot moves to the heel.

Keeping the head motionless, or steady, and behind the ball throughout the swing is the key to solid contact. If golfers want to hit the ball hard, Palmer advises, "Once you can keep your head steady,…hit it as hard as you want."[98] However, we hit hard at the bottom of the swing arc; we do not ever swing hard from the top.

We should let the rotation of the hips and the change in down pressure to the front foot initiate the downswing. This action starts prior to the completion of the backswing and is an integral part of the transition. The rotation of the hips to the front begins the pull on the left arm. The left arm controls the swing arc as it increases in speed. The right arm moves down and in toward the side. The rotation of the shoulders does not begin immediately, but lags behind the rotation of the hips. This lag by the shoulders allows the club to be pulled toward the horizontal by hip rotation. The lag in the shoulder turn creates more torque.

The shoulders begin to turn as the hands approach horizontal, and the wrists begin to uncock as the club passes horizontal. This lag allows the second pendulum of the wrist cock to add speed to the primary pendulum.

At or near the bottom of the swing arc, the clubface strikes the ball. (With the driver, this strike can happen on the upswing.) Leading into the ball strike, the left arm is fully extended while the right arm remains partially bent. This allows the right arm to add power to the swing. The right arm and hand take over as the club strikes the ball, even though we hit hard with both hands, and the right hand pronates through the release. The club is extended toward the target and both arms are temporarily fully extended. The left arm folds back to the side while the right arm extends out and up for a high finish.

The Downswing Wrap-up

1. Heavy down pressure is moved to the front foot.
2. Hips are rotated to the front, followed by the shoulders, arms, and hands.
3. The wrists remain cocked until the clubhead drops below horizontal in order to keep the double pendulum in line with the ball-target line.
4. The uncocking of the wrists begins as the club drops below the horizontal, continues through the ball strike, and ends with the release. The release refers to the natural rotation of the wrists that is part of the follow-through.
5. The right hand ends with extended palm down toward the target.
6. The downswing finishes with the hands high over the left shoulder.

Part V

16
The Golf Ball

We cannot play the game without a ball, and we have all witnessed balls doing unpredictable, even unexplainable, things now and then. This behavior is often attributed to sheer dumb luck, but we should remember that golf balls are designed and produced to have predictable behavior. They are made to exacting manufacturing specifications, and all golfers can trust that these dimpled, round spheres are exact replicas of prototypes that passed the distance and spin tests identified in the sales promotion. The golf ball is controlled by the USGA, and rules specify a maximum weight of 1.62 ounces, a determined size of nothing less than 1.680 inches in diameter, spherical symmetry, and initial velocity of not more than two hundred fifty feet per second; the combined carry and roll of the ball must not exceed the distance specified on file with the USGA.

With these specifications in mind, what magic allows some manufacturers to tell us that their balls fly farther and spin better than the competition? The answer, of course, is design. There are balls with solid cores, and there are balls with two-, three-, and four-piece construction along with different dimple designs ranging from three hundred to more than four hundred dimples that account for variabilities in distance and spin. Balls are tested, and the results show differences in performance due to the number of layers around the core, the outside cover design, and material. Most golfers would benefit by doing real research on the ball.

The primary concern for beginners and high handicappers is probably hitting the ball long and straight. In this case, those golfers should choose a two-piece ball. There are a number of quality, low-spin, distance golf balls designed specifically to reduce the sidespin that exaggerates slices and hooks; they can help produce longer, straighter drives. For middle to low handicappers with a fast swing speed, the key to improvement (like consistently breaking eighty) will be better pitches, chips, and putting. In this case, golfers should move to a multi-layer ball. These balls have the thinner cover, and the core layers give golfers more feel and higher spin rates.

Swing speed is an important element in determining which ball or club shaft golfers should choose. Golfers can find out what their swing speed is by getting it measured electronically, or they can keep track of their driving distance (carry and roll) and divide that number by 2.5 (two hundred yards divided by 2.5 equals a swing speed of eighty miles per hour). It is simple to get a good estimate of swing speed by using this formula, but we should all keep in mind that an electronic measurement will be more exact.

In deciding which ball to purchase, golfers should know that equipment is only about 10 percent of the game, and the ball represents only a portion of that 10 percent. The most expensive balls may be a necessary element in the games of low-handicap golfers and professionals, but for the majority of golfers the cost benefit analysis does not pay off. The basic truth being that golf balls fly straight and long off the tee and spin and stop on the green because of the skills of the golfer, not by some hidden magic built into the ball by the manufacturer. My advice is to take the money to the practice range and leave the high-dollar balls to the low handicappers and professionals.

Each year 1.2 billion closely related members of the golf ball family are produced for a worldwide golfing community of about fifty-five million. That is equal to almost two dozen golf balls per player. Why so many? In the United States alone, it is estimated that more than three hundred million of those balls have gone astray and are lost each year. That's a high mortality rate. Based on an estimated average cost of two dollars per ball, that comes to a staggering six hundred million dollars hiding in the woods, rough, and water hazards of United States' golf courses every year.

To the average golfer, the golf balls he or she plays with will never become close to their hearts like their clubs, the killer putter, a special golf hat, or the favorite ball mark. Some golfers believe that if they play the very best ball, it gives them an advantage even though they are not skilled enough to capitalize on the characteristics of the ball they play. The fact is that a poorly struck high-priced ball will misbehave just as quickly as the lower-cost ball, and, in some cases, it will misbehave even quicker. What should we do? Purchasing a lower-cost ball might lead to more time on the practice range. Golfers should consider finding a ball that has performance characteristics that fit their games, their psyches, and their pocketbooks.

In general, lower-cost, two-piece balls travel farther. Low spin rates equal greater distance with drives as the ball will roll farther when it hits the fairway. These balls are also easier to control off the tee because of less spin, but the lower spin rates make them harder to control around the green. High spin rates are valuable if a golfer is skilled enough to work the ball. If a golfer's game is not highly controlled, the less expensive ball seems an obvious choice.

Once we own a ball that fits our game and pocketbook, what can we do to make certain that it will perform to our expectations? It would seem obvious, but the first rule is to keep the ball clean. Between the tee and the hole, there are rules governing when golfers can lift and clean their balls. It is important to know these rules. The most advanced dimple design will be of no benefit if the ball is dirty.

One final piece of playing advice is to hit the ball hard. Not one of the professionals we studied advised us to hit the ball with an easy swing. Just because Sam Snead has the sweetest swing doesn't mean he's not hitting hard. A sweet swing, a swing smooth as butter—both can be hard swings. The consensus among the Legends is that it is easier to learn control over a hard-hit ball than it would be to learn to swing hard once a golfer has developed a pattern of swinging easy. Golfers should trust the fundamentals, trust their swing, and swing hard from the start.

17
Closing Advice

We've discussed several topics in this book, some old and some new, and all, I hope, helpful in the quest to play better golf. I've discussed the fundamentals as presented by the seven Legends. I've talked about how the brain works to absorb information and build motor skills, especially in adult learners. I have stressed the most important ingredient in the game of golf: self-confidence, which cannot exist without trust.

Hundreds of golf books have been written with theories about how golfers should think and perform on the golf course, and there are thousands of books about performance in sports and in business. The conclusion one reaches from studying these books is that self-confidence is a major key to success. Building self-confidence is achieved through increased knowledge, preparation, and successful performance. But when a crisis comes—and it will—on the golf course, we need to have a strong sense of trust in our game. Doom is just a tee shot away, and, as Bobby Jones so aptly described the problem, "One reason golf is such an exasperating game is that a thing learned is so easily forgotten, and we find ourselves struggling year after year with faults we had discovered and corrected time and again."[99] Mistakes in what we do cause errors in how we hit the ball, and errors cause doubt. We all know that when we start doubting ourselves, the simple chip shot or three-foot putt seem nearly impossible; that doubt comes from a lack of trust in our game.

Now walk with me back in time to the five-hundred-yard line at the rifle range at Quantico. The pressure was on, and I had already made many mistakes. I knew I was not shooting up to the potential I had shown in practice. At that moment, I could either decide that the skills I had practiced were insufficient and that the knowledge I had was failing me and try to figure out another way to score better, or I could decide to trust fully in those skills, in the knowledge I had acquired, and in all my practice hours, and put them to work for me. I chose the latter option: trust. In doing so, I bet my success on the teachings of the Marine Corps instructors of the Quantico rifle range. My practice and my knowledge were sufficient for the task at hand, so I had to stay out of my head and trust that my training had prepared me.

The only purpose for this book is to help golfers become the best golfers they are capable of becoming. That success is dependent on each one of us. Knowledge without practice will fail under pressure. When we practice, that is the time to think, and that process develops and improves skill habits. When we play, that is the time to allow the unconscious to take over.

The use of the seven Legends as the backbone of this book had one simple reason. Their achievements speak for themselves, and golfers the world over can have total trust in their teachings even when errors happen or when we make mistakes.

When we make errors, we should try to forget them because errors happen to everyone who plays the game. Focusing on mistakes erodes self-confidence. Putting errors behind us is a lesson all good golfers must learn. Bobby Jones was happy when he hit six good shots in a round. Golf is a difficult game to learn and to play—maybe the most difficult game there is. Statistics show us that the guys who play golf for a living only hit six out of ten fairways in regulation. On approach shots, they are a bit more accurate, averaging 65 percent success, and on sand saves they average one out of two. This is why the Legends agree that we cannot ever master golf, only continue to improve, so the next time we miss a fairway, a green, or can't get up and down from the trap, we need to remember that misses are part of the game.

Our success in performing skills well under pressure more often than we make errors requires that we trust our sources of knowledge, we trust in our ability to have acquired and maintained those skills, and we allow ourselves to strike the ball without conscious cognitive interruption. Trust is the foundation of self-confidence. We should all remember what Vince Lombardi says, "The man on top of the mountain didn't fall there."

Endnotes

1 Sam Snead, *Sam Snead Teaches You His Simple "KEY" Approach to Golf,* with Larry Sheehan (New York: Atheneum, 1975), 5.

2 Robert Tyre Jones, Jr., *Golf Is My Game* (London: A & C Black, 1990), *49.*

3 Sam Snead, *Sam Snead Teaches You His Simple "KEY" Approach to Golf,* with Larry Sheehan (New York: Atheneum, 1975), 5.

4 Ibid.

5 H. L. Mencken, "The Divine Afflatus," *New York Evening Mail*, November 16, 1917.

6 Robert Tyre Jones, Jr., *Bobby Jones on Golf* (New York: Broadway Books, 2001), xvii.

7 Ben Hogan, *Five Lessons: The Modern Fundamentals of Golf,* with Herbert Warren Wind (New York: Simon & Schuster, 1985), 17.

8 Bob Cullen, *Why Golf?: The Mystery of the Game Revisited* (New York: Simon & Schuster, 2000), 23.

9 Ben Hogan, *Five Lessons: The Modern Fundamentals of Golf,* with Herbert Warren Wind (New York: Simon & Schuster, 1985), 37.

10 *The Legend of Bagger Vance*, directed by Robert Redford. (Universal City, CA: DreamWorks Productions, 2000). Full-length film.

11 Arnold Palmer, My *Game and Yours* (New York: Simon & Schuster, 1965), 12.

12 Jack Nicklaus, *Jack Nicklaus' Playing Lessons,* with Ken Bowden (Norwalk, CT: Golf Digest, 1981), 123.

13 Robert Tyre Jones, Jr., *Bobby Jones on Golf* (New York: Broadway Books, 2001), xi.

14 Arnold Palmer, My *Game and Yours* (New York: Simon & Schuster, 1965), 9.

15 Ibid., 10.

16 Richard Brody, "Why We Care (and Don't Care) About the New Rules of Golf, *New Yorker,* January 29, 2019.

17 Robert Tyre Jones, Jr., *Golf Is My Game* (London: A & C Black, 1990), 72.

18 Harvey Penick, *And If You Play Golf, You're My Friend: Further Reflections of a Grown Caddie,* with Bud Shrake (New York: Simon & Schuster, 1993), 172.

19 Harvey Penick, *Harvey Penick's Little Red Book: Lessons and Teachings from a Lifetime in Golf*, with Bud Shrake (New York: Simon & Schuster, 1992), 172.

20 Robert Tyre Jones, Jr., *Bobby Jones on Golf* (New York: Broadway Books, 2001), 35.

21 Ben Hogan, *Five Lessons: The Modern Fundamentals of Golf*, with Herbert Warren Wind (New York: Simon & Schuster, 1985), 37.

22 Tom Watson, *The Timeless Swing*, with Nick Seitz (New York: Atria Books, 2011), 12.

23 Sam Snead, *Golf Begins at Forty: How to Use Your Age Advantage*, with Dick Aultman (New York: Doubleday, 1978), 171.

24 Ibid., 12,171.

25 Ibid., 171.

26 Arnold Palmer, *My Game and Yours*, rev. ed. (New York: Simon & Schuster, 1983), 12.

27 Mortimer J. Adler, *How to Think About The Great Ideas* (Peru, IL: Open Court, 2002), 179.

28 David Eagleman, *Incognito: The Secret Lives of the Brain* (New York: Pantheon, 2011), 4.

29 Ibid, 4.

30 Ibid., 74.

31 Jeffrey T. Fairbrother, *Fundamentals of Motor Behavior* (Champaign, IL: Human Kinetics, 2010), 45.

32 Robert Tyre Jones, Jr., *Bobby Jones on Golf* (New York: Broadway Books, 2001), 11.

33 Eliezer J. Sternberg, *Neurologic: The Brain's Hidden Rationale Behind Our Irrational Behavior* (New York: Vintage Books, 2015), 78.

34 Ibid., 75.

35 Jack Nicklaus, *Golf My Way*, with Ken Bowden (New York: Simon & Schuster, 1974), 22.

36 Robert Tyre Jones, Jr., *Bobby Jones on Golf* (New York: Broadway Books, 2001), 8.

37 Ben Hogan, *Five Lessons: The Modern Fundamentals of Golf*, with Herbert Warren Wind (New York: Simon & Schuster, 1985), 18.

38 Sam Snead, *Sam Snead on Golf* (Englewood Cliffs, NJ: Prentice-Hall, 1961), 27.

39 Arnold Palmer, *My Game and Yours*, rev. ed. (New York: Simon & Schuster, 1983), 13.

40 Tom Watson, *Tom Watson's Getting Back to Basics*, with Nick Seitz (Trumbull, CT: Golf Digest/ Pocket Books, 1992), 22.

41 Harvey Penick, *Harvey Penick's Little Red Book: Lessons and Teachings from a Lifetime in Golf*, with Bud Shrake (New York: Simon & Schuster, 1992), 30.

42 Jack Nicklaus, *The Full Swing*, with Ken Bowden (Trumball, CT: Golf Digest, 1984), 28.

43 Arnold Palmer, *My Game and Yours*, rev. ed. (New York: Simon & Schuster, 1983), 13.

44 Tom Watson, *The Timeless Swing*, with Nick Seitz (New York: Atria Books, 2011), 14.

45 Sam Snead, *Sam Snead Teaches You His Simple "KEY" Approach to Golf*, with Larry Sheehan (New York: Atheneum, 1975), 44.

46 Sam Snead, *Sam Snead Teaches You His Simple "KEY" Approach to Golf*, with Larry Sheehan (New York: Atheneum, 1975), 44.

47 Ben Hogan, *Five Lessons: The Modern Fundamentals of Golf*, with Herbert Warren Wind (New York: Simon & Schuster, 1985), 33.

48 Tom Watson, *The Timeless Swing*, with Nick Seitz (New York: Atria Books, 2011), 28.

49 Jack Nicklaus, *Golf My Way*, with Ken Bowden (New York: Simon & Schuster, 1974), 71.

50 Robert Tyre Jones, Jr., *Golf Is My Game* (London: A & C Black, 1990), 49.

51 Jack Nicklaus, *My Golden Lessons: 100-Plus Ways to Improve Your Shots, Lower Your Scores, and Enjoy Golf Much, Much More*, with Ken Bowden (New York: Simon & Schuster, 2002), 73.

52 Tom Watson, *The Timeless Swing*, with Nick Seitz (New York: Atria Books, 2011), 29.

53 Robert Tyre Jones, Jr., *Golf Is My Game* (London: A & C Black, 1990), 48.

54 Sam Snead, *Golf Begins at Forty: How to Use Your Age Advantage*, with Dick Aultman (New York: Doubleday, 1978), 76.

55 Arnold Palmer, *My Game and Yours*, rev. ed. (New York: Simon & Schuster, 1983), 17.

56 Jack Nicklaus, *My Golden Lessons: 100-Plus Ways to Improve Your Shots, Lower Your Scores, and Enjoy Golf Much, Much More*, with Ken Bowden (New York: Simon & Schuster, 2002), 33.

57 Arnold Palmer, *Play Great Golf: Mastering the Fundamentals of Your Game* (Garden City, NY: Doubleday, 1987), 11.

58 Sam Snead, *Sam Snead Teaches You His Simple "KEY" Approach to Golf*, with Larry Sheehan (New York: Atheneum, 1975), 44.

59 Arnold Palmer, *Play Great Golf: Mastering the Fundamentals of Your Game* (Garden City, NY: Doubleday, 1987), 24.

60 Jack Nicklaus, *My Golden Lessons: 100-Plus Ways to Improve Your Shots, Lower Your Scores, and Enjoy Golf Much, Much More*, with Ken Bowden (New York: Simon & Schuster, 2002), 29.

61 Jack Nicklaus, *Golf My Way*, with Ken Bowden (New York: Simon & Schuster, 1974), 79.

62 Ibid., 35.

63 Jack Nicklaus, *My Golden Lessons: 100-Plus Ways to Improve Your Shots, Lower Your Scores, and Enjoy Golf Much, Much More*, with Ken Bowden (New York: Simon & Schuster, 2002), 29.

64 Tom Watson, *The Timeless Swing*, with Nick Seitz (New York: Atria Books, 2011), xii.

65 Sam Snead, *Sam Snead Teaches You His Simple "KEY" Approach to Golf*, with Larry Sheehan (New York: Atheneum, 1975), 9.

66 Sam Snead, *Sam Snead on Golf* (Englewood Cliffs, NJ: Prentice-Hall, 1961), 128.

67 Sam Snead, *The Game I Love: Wisdom, Insight, and Instruction from Golf's Greatest Player*, with Fran Pirozzolo (New York: Ballantine Books, 1997), 132.

68 Harvey Penick, *And If You Play Golf, You're My Friend: Further Reflections of a Grown Caddie*, with Bud Shrake (New York: Simon & Schuster, 1993), 60.

69 Harvey Penick, *Harvey Penick's Little Red Book: Lessons and Teachings from a Lifetime in Golf*, with Bud Shrake (New York: Simon & Schuster, 1992), 75.

70 Robert Tyre Jones, Jr., *Golf Is My Game* (London: A & C Black, 1990), 50.

71 Jack Nicklaus, *The Full Swing*, with Ken Bowden (Trumball, CT: Golf Digest, 1984), 56.

72 Tom Watson, *The Timeless Swing*, with Nick Seitz (New York: Atria Books, 2011), 34.

73 Sam Snead, *Sam Snead Teaches You His Simple "KEY" Approach to Golf*, with Larry Sheehan (New York: Atheneum, 1975), 31.

74 Ben Hogan, *Five Lessons: The Modern Fundamentals of Golf*, with Herbert Warren Wind (New York: Simon & Schuster, 1985), 39.

75 Harvey Penick, *Harvey Penick's Little Red Book: Lessons and Teachings from a Lifetime in Golf*, with Bud Shrake (New York: Simon & Schuster, 1992), 111.

76 Jack Nicklaus, *My Golden Lessons: 100-Plus Ways to Improve Your Shots, Lower Your Scores, and Enjoy Golf Much, Much More*, with Ken Bowden (New York: Simon & Schuster, 2002), 42.

77 Sam Snead, *Sam Snead Teaches You His Simple "KEY" Approach to Golf*, with Larry Sheehan (New York: Atheneum, 1975), 52.

78 Ibid.

79 Ben Hogan, *Five Lessons: The Modern Fundamentals of Golf*, with Herbert Warren Wind (New York: Simon & Schuster, 1985), 41-42.

80 Ibid, 45.

81 Harvey Penick, *The Game for a Lifetime: More Lessons and Teachings*, with Bud Shrake (New York: Simon & Schuster, 1996), 46.

82 Harvey Penick, *Harvey Penick's Little Red Book: Lessons and Teachings from a Lifetime in Golf*, with Bud Shrake (New York: Simon & Schuster, 1992), 47.

83 Arnold Palmer, *Play Great Golf: Mastering the Fundamentals of Your Game* (Garden City, NY: Doubleday, 1987), 25.

84 Sam Snead, *Better Golf the Sam Snead Way: The Lessons I've Learned* (Chicago: Contemporary Books, 1989), 11.

85 Harvey Penick, *Harvey Penick's Little Red Book: Lessons and Teachings from a Lifetime in Golf*, with Bud Shrake (New York: Simon & Schuster, 1992), 81.

86 Sam Snead, *Sam Snead Teaches You His Simple "KEY" Approach to Golf*, with Larry Sheehan (New York: Atheneum, 1975), 73.

87 Robert Tyre Jones, Jr., *Golf Is My Game* (London: A & C Black, 1990), 52.

88 Ibid, 55

89 Jack Nicklaus, *Golf My Way*, with Ken Bowden (New York: Simon & Schuster, 1974), 101.

90 Tom Watson, *The Timeless Swing*, with Nick Seitz (New York: Atria Books, 2011), 65.

91 Ibid, 69.

92 Harvey Penick, *For All Who Love the Game: Lessons and Teachings for Women*, with Bud Shrake (New York: Simon & Schuster, 1995), 50.

93 Jack Nicklaus, *My Golden Lessons: 100-Plus Ways to Improve Your Shots, Lower Your Scores, and Enjoy Golf Much, Much More*, with Ken Bowden (New York: Simon & Schuster, 2002), 56.

94 Robert Tyre Jones, Jr., *Golf Is My Game* (London: A & C Black, 1990), 57.

95 Arnold Palmer, *Play Great Golf: Mastering the Fundamentals of Your Game* (Garden City, NY: Doubleday, 1987), 44.

96 Bob Mullen, *Golf from the Ground Up* (Short Hills, NJ: Burford Books Inc, 2009), 101.

97 Ben Hogan, *Five Lessons: The Modern Fundamentals of Golf,* with Herbert Warren Wind (New York: Simon & Schuster, 1985), 99.

98 Arnold Palmer, *Play Great Golf: Mastering the Fundamentals of Your Game* (Garden City, NY: Doubleday, 1987), 42.

99 Robert Tyre Jones, Jr., *Bobby Jones on Golf,* (New York: Broadway Books, 2001), 35.

Glossary

aiming. The act of aligning the clubface to the target.

address. The position the golfer puts his or her body into prior to making the swing. Part of the preshot routine. Same as setup.

alignment. The position of the body in relation to the target.

approach. A shot hit toward the green.

arc. A part of circle; the path followed by the swing of the golf club.

axis. The line (the spine) that the body rotates or winds around during the course of the golf swing.

axon. A long and single nerve-cell projection that conducts impulses away from the cell body.

backspin. The rotational movement or spin of the ball produced by contact with the clubface. The greater the backspin, the higher the ball will fly and the more it will spin and stop or even spin backward on impact with the turf.

backswing. The motion that involves taking the club away from the ball and setting it in the slot at the topmost position of the swing prior to making the downswing.

balance. Proper distribution of weight during setup and throughout the swing.

ball-target line. An imaginary line that runs through the ball to the target.

birdie. A score of one under par on a hole.

block practice. A type of practice that involves one task repeated again and again.

blocked shot. An action that happens during the swing in which the rotation of the forearms is delayed or prevented throughout the hitting area, generally producing a shot that flies to the right of the target.

bogey, bogie. A score of one over par on a hole.

bunker. Also **sand trap**; A hollow comprised of sand or grass or both that exists as an obstacle and, in some cases, as a hazard.

carry. The distance a ball will fly in the air.

center of mass (COM). A point representing the mean position of the mean position of the matter in a body.

centrifugal force. The action in a rotating body that tends to move mass away from the center. It is the force a golfer feels in the downswing that pulls the clubhead outward and downward, extending the arms and encouraging them to take a circular path.

centripetal force. The force that is necessary to keep an object moving in a curved path and that is directed inward toward the center of rotation.

chunk. A poor shot caused by hitting the turf behind the ball, resulting in what is called a fat shot.

closed clubface. A position during the swing in which the direction of the clubface is angled to the inside of the target line, generally resulting in shots hit to the left of the target.

closed stance. A description of the position of a golfer's feet when the rear foot is pulled back away from the target line.

closed-to-open. A swing in which the clubhead is closed on the backswing, but then manipulated into an open position on the downswing.

cock and uncock. (See **wrist cock** and **wrist uncock**.)

coil. The turning of the body during the backswing.

cupping (the wrists or hands). Refers to the action of the hands when trying to loft a ball toward the target. Involves **extension** and **flexion** of the wrists during the swing and is considered a golfing no-no.

divot. The turf displaced when the club strikes the ball on a descending path. It also refers to the hole left after play.

double pendulum. The two-part movement of the golf club during the swing; the first pendulum is the big arc of the arm swing. The second pendulum is a smaller arc made as the wrists are cocked and uncocked, adding velocity to the overall speed of the clubhead. These two arcs must be aligned to achieve an effective swing.

downswing. The movement of the club occurring after transition, moving the club on a downward path to contact the ball.

draw. A shot that flies slightly from right to left for right-handed players.

driving range. Another term for a practice area. Also known as a golf range, practice range, or learning center.

dynamic balance. Maintaining body control by appropriate management of weight, which allows the swing arc to stay unchanged.

extension. Movement of the palm of the hand away from the inside of the wrist. In golf it occurs simultaneously with flexion of the opposite hand. Often referred to as cupping the wrists and is a golfing no-no.

fade. A shot designed to follow a ball-target line to the left of the intended target, but with left-to-right spin sufficient to turn it to the right and toward the target as it reaches the green or appropriate area of the fairway.

fat shot. A shot in which the clubhead strikes the turf behind the ball, resulting in poor contact and a shot that comes up well short of the target.

flat stance. Allows the golfer to rotate the shoulders, core, and hips in the same plane as the swing. The swing is flatter or more horizontal and easier to generate swing speed, but because the arc is flatter, the clubhead does not stay in the hitting zone as long as it does in the upright swing.

flexion. Movement of the palm of the hand toward the inside of the wrist. It occurs simultaneously with extension of the opposite hand on the golf club. Often referred to as cupping the wrists and is a golfing no-no.

fly. The distance the ball carries in the air.

follow-through. The finish of the swing, occurring after the ball has been struck and simultaneously with the release.

footwork. The coordinated action of the feet during the golf swing. The feet do not remain fixed during the swing.

forward press. A slight movement of the hands and arms (and occasionally the legs) that initiate the golf swing. It can be toward or away from the target.

frontal cortex. The part of the brain where conscious thinking, remembering, and reasoning occurs. The frontal lobes are responsible for initiating motor function, problem solving, spontaneity, memory, language, judgement, impulse control, and social and sexual behavior.

Glossary

fundamentals. The basic golf skills that, when combined, make up the golf swing. Sometimes referred to as the mechanics of the swing.

golf range. A facility where people can practice their full swings and, in some cases, their short games.

grand slam. The modern (or professional) grand slam describes winning the four professional major championships—the PGA Championship, the Masters, the United States Open, and the British Open—in a single calendar year. The career grand slam describes winning each of these events once in a career. Only Gene Sarazen, Ben Hogan, Gary Player, Jack Nicklaus, and Tiger Woods have accomplished this. No one has ever won the modern grand slam. In 1930, Bobby Jones won the United States Open, British Open, and both amateur opens, termed the grand slam at that time and has never been duplicated. The twenty-eight-year-old Jones retired from competitive golf that year. .

grip. (1) The part on the golf club where the hands are placed. (2) Also called the hold, which refers to the placing and positioning of the hands on the club.

ground. When referred to in the rules of golf, it means the point when the club touches the ground (or water) prior to playing the shot.

hooding. The act of placing the hands ahead of the ball, both at address and impact, which tends to reduce the effective loft of the club.

hold. Refers to the placing and positioning of the hands on the club.

hook. A shot that curves sharply from right to left for right-handed players.

hosel. The portion of the clubhead where the clubhead curves and is attached to the shaft.

impact. The moment in the swing when the club strikes the ball.

inside-to-in. A description of the swing path that should produce the greatest percentage of solid, straight, and on-target shots. It refers to a path in which the clubhead travels from inside the target line to impact and then back inside the target line.

inside-to-out. A swing path in which the clubhead approaches the ball from inside the target line and, after contact, continues along the ball-target line before turning back to the inside in the follow-through.

interlocking. In golf, this always refers to a grip or hold where the little finger of one hand is linked to the inside of the index finger of the other hand.

kinesiology. The scientific study of man's movement and the movements of implements or equipment that he might use in exercise, sport, or other forms of physical activity.

lag. A shot (usually a pitch, chip, or putt) designed to finish short of the target.

lateral slide or shift. A movement during the swing in which the hips slide toward the target rather than rotate around the body axis. This movement can shift the COM ahead of the ball at impact.

Laura's Law. Eighty percent of the weight must be transferred to the lead foot prior to the beginning of the golf swing to avoid the out-to-in swing path. Degrees off center = arc tan (x in/66 in)*57 deg/rad, where the pendulum arc = arm and club, and x = length in inches between person's belly button and front leg.

lie. (1) As it relates to the ball, the position of the ball when it has come to rest. (2) As it relates to the club, the angle of the sole of the club relative to the shaft.

line. The intended path of the ball following a stroke (the ball target line).

loft. The degree of angle on the clubface related to the shaft, with the least loft on a putter and the most on a lob wedge.

long irons. The one to three irons.

looking up. The act of prematurely lifting the head to follow the flight of the ball, which also raises the swing center and can result in erratic ball striking.

loosening the grip. Any time during the swing that the player opens his fingers and loses control of the club. This often happens at the top of the backswing.

mantra. A sound, word, or combination of words said by a golfer, silently or aloud, just before he or she begins the backswing. It is intended to release the conscious mind and place the control of the shot in the subconscious or motor cortex.

middle or midirons. The four to seven irons. An iron golf club with more loft than a driving iron and less than a wedge, used typically for medium-distance shots on the fairway and long-approach shots from the fairway.

motionless head. Keeping the head still and behind the ball during the swing avoids many golf errors.

neuron. A grayish or reddish granular cell that is the fundamental functional unit of nervous tissue transmitting and receiving nerve impulses. Attached to the neuron are dendrites, which have many axons extending from them, and these together direct the nerve impulses to different muscles in the body.

neuron bundle. Created as the frontal cortex recruits many neurons to send specific messages to the motor cortex. Once firmly established, these bundles will allow the motor cortex to perform the given function without the frontal cortex being involved.

one-piece takeaway. Sometimes called the modern takeaway, it describes the beginning of the backswing when the hands, arms, and wrists move away from the ball simultaneously while maintaining the same relationship they had at address.

open clubface. When, either at address or during the swing, the heel of the clubhead is leading the toe, causing the clubface to point to the side of the target.

open stance. When the lead foot is pulled back farther from the target line than the rear foot. This stance generally helps promote a left-to-right ball flight.

open-to-closed. A description of the movement of the clubface when a player fans it open on the backswing and then closes it at impact.

outside-to-in. A description of a swing path when the clubhead approaches the ball from outside the target line and then continues to the inside of that line following impact.

par. The score an accomplished player is expected to make on a hole—either a three, four, or five.

palm's heel. The raised portion of the palm just below the wrist.

path. The direction the club travels during the swing or the putting stroke. Sometimes called a swing path or arc.

pendulum. Something that swings suspended from a fixed point so as to move freely back and forth at regular intervals; used to regulate movements.

pitching wedge. A type of golf club used for hitting a golf ball so it goes very high in the air and rolls very little after it hits the ground.

preshot routine. The actions a player takes from the time he selects a club until he begins the swing. This routine should become a habit and be used before every shot. It is a critical step in preparing to swing the club.

pronation. A simultaneous inward rotation of the forearm and hand so that the palm faces backward or downward.. In golf, for a right-handed golfer, it describes the rotation of the right forearm and hand through the impact area and the finish.

pulled hook. A shot that begins to the inside of the target line and continues to curve even farther away.

pulled shot. A relatively straight shot that begins to the inside of the target and doesn't curve back.

pulled slice. A shot that starts well to the side of the target, but curves back to the target.

push off. An attempt to increase distance by pushing off the back foot instead of transferring weight to the front foot and rotating. The push off is generally accompanied by the slide or lateral movement of the hips. This results in an out-to-in swing path and a slice or pull.

pushed hook. A shot that begins to the outside of the target, but curves back toward the target.

pushed shot. A shot that starts to the outside of the target and never curves back.

pushed slice. A shot that starts to the outside of the target and curves farther away.

reading the green (or putt). The entire process involved in judging the break and path of a putt.

release. Release is the pronation of the right forearm and supination of the left forearm. This is natural swing action. The right palm rolls from vertical to a down position. Simultaneously bottom left palm supinates (move to the palm up position). Understanding this will add distance and power to your shots and may eventually find that your slice becomes a draw. Relax your forearms and allow them to rotate as you hit through the ball at impact. Exactly opposite for left handed golfers.

rhythm. The coordination of movement during the golf swing or putting stroke.

rotation. This refers to the coiling and uncoiling action of the body during the swing, which adds power to the swing.

sand trap. Also **bunker**; an artificial hazard on a golf course consisting of a depression filled with sand.

sand wedge. A golfing iron with considerable loft and a wide flange for use in blasting from a sand trap.

setup. The position the golfer puts his or her body in prior to making the swing. It is part of the preshot routine and the same as addressing the ball.

shaft. The long handle of a golf club.

shank. When the ball is struck on the hosel of the club, usually sending it shooting off to the right.

shape. To curve a shot to fit the situation; this word is also used to describe the flight of the ball.

short game. Those shots played on and around the green, including putting, chipping, pitching, and bunker shots.

short irons. The eight and nine irons and the wedges.

slice. A ball that curves from left to right during flight. Generally, not a controlled shot but one hit by improper fundamentals.

slot. The position of the hands and clubhead at the top of the backswing arc. The length of the arc can vary with the length of the club or type of shot being played but the arc is the same for all clubs.

square. A term frequently used in golf. It can be used to refer to the alignment of a golfer's stance, the position of the clubface, or contact with the ball. It can also refer to the status of a tied match.

stance. The position of the feet, legs, hips, shoulders, and hands to allow for a free and balanced uninterrupted swing.

supination. A rotation of the forearm and hand so that the palm faces forward and upward. In the golf swing for a right-handed golfer, it describes the rotation of the left forearm and hand through the impact area and the finish.

swing arc. The entire path the clubhead makes in the course of a swing. It is a combination of the swing's width and length.

swing plane. An imaginary surface that describes the path and angle of the club during the swing.

takeaway. The beginning of the backswing describing the movement of the club away from the ball until it reaches almost horizontal.

tee box. The area from which a golf ball is struck at the beginning of a hole. The term evolved from the early days of golf before wooden tees when golfers actually used a box filled with sand to make a tee at the starting point of each hole.

tempo. The speed of the swing action, not necessarily the clubhead speed.

ten-finger grip. A manner of holding the club such that all ten fingers are placed on the club. Also known as a baseball grip.

timing. Sequence of motions within the golf swing. They must occur in order and be of the proper duration to be effective. The term timing is used to describe this achievement.

transition. The point at which the golf swing changes direction between the backswing and the downswing. In some swings, there is a brief pause during the transition.

upright stance. A more vertical stance, giving the golfer more control because the swing arc is on the ball-target line for a longer period of time. However, the upright golfer has to deal with shoulders and hips that rotate on a different plane than the swing.

Vardon or overlapping grip. A particular way to place the hands on the golf club in which the little finger of the right hand rests on top of the index finger of the left hand (for right-handed golfers; the reverse is true for left-handed golfers) and is used by about 80 percent of golfers today.

visualization. Creating a mental image of a swing or shot prior to making a shot. This can be done as a practice procedure without actually playing. The mental picture should include the setup, the shot, and the flight of the ball.

waggle. A motion or several motions designed to keep a player relaxed at address and help establish a smooth pace in the takeaway and swing.

wrist cock. To bend the wrist toward the thumb in preparation of swinging the club. This action is distinct from flexion and extension in that cocking refers to the bending of the wrists toward the thumb (cocking) and away from the thumb toward the little finger (uncocking). Flexion and extension refer to the bending of the wrists toward (flexion) and away from (extension) the palm of the hand.

Bibliography

Golf

Apfelbaum, Jim, ed. *The Gigantic Book of Golf Quotations.* New York: Skyhorse Publishing, 2007.

Cullen, Bob. *Why Golf?: The Mystery of the Game Revisited.* New York: Simon & Schuster, 2000.

Hogan, Ben. *Ben Hogan's Power Golf: A Proven Method to Reduce Your Score.* New York: Pocket Books, 1957.

Hogan, Ben. *Five Lessons: The Modern Fundamentals of Golf.* With Herbert Warren Wind. New York: Simon & Schuster, 1985. First published 1957 by Cornerstone Library.

Jones, Robert Tyre, Jr. *Bobby Jones on Golf.* New York: Broadway Books, 2001. First published 1966 by Doubleday.

Jones, Robert Tyre, Jr. *Golf Is My Game.* London: A & C Black, 1990. First published 1961 by Chatto & Windus.

Jones, Robert Tyre, Jr. and O. B. Keeler. *Down the Fairway.* New York: British American Publishing, 2005. First published 1927 by Milton, Balch.

Matthew, Sidney L., ed. *Bobby Jones Golf Tips.* Chelsea, MI: Sleeping Bear Press, 1999.

Nicklaus, Jack. *The Full Swing.* With Ken Bowden. Trumball, CT: Golf Digest, 1984.

Nicklaus, Jack. *Golf My Way.* With Ken Bowden. New York: Simon & Schuster, 1974.

Nicklaus, Jack. *Jack Nicklaus' Lesson Tee.* With Ken Bowden. Norwalk, CT: Golf Digest, 1977.

Nicklaus, Jack. *Jack Nicklaus' Playing Lessons.* With Ken Bowden. Norwalk, CT: Golf Digest, 1981.

Nicklaus, Jack. *My Golden Lessons: 100-Plus Ways to Improve Your Shots, Lower Your Scores, and Enjoy Golf Much, Much More.* With Ken Bowden. New York: Simon & Schuster, 2002.

Nicklaus, Jack. *Play Better Golf: Short Cuts to Lower Scores.* With Ken Bowden. New York: Pocket Books, 1983.

Nicklaus, Jack. *Play Better Golf: The Short Game and Scoring.* With Ken Bowden. New York: Pocket Books, 1981.

Bibliography

Nicklaus, Jack. *Play Better Golf: The Swing from A-Z*. With Ken Bowden. New York: Pocket Books, 1980

Nicklaus, Jack. *Putting My Way: A Lifetime's Worth of Tips from Golf's All-time Greatest*. With Ken Bowden. Hoboken, NJ: John Wiley & Sons, 2009.

Palmer, Arnold and Peter Dobereiner. *Arnold Palmer's Complete Book of Putting*. New York: Atheneum, 1986.

Palmer, Arnold. *My Game and Yours*. New York: Simon & Schuster, 1965.

Palmer, Arnold. *My Game and Yours*, rev. ed. New York: Simon & Schuster, 1983.

Palmer, Arnold. *Play Great Golf: Mastering the Fundamentals of Your Game*. Garden City, NY: Doubleday, 1987.

Penick, Harvey. *And If You Play Golf, You're My Friend: Further Reflections of a Grown Caddie*. With Bud Shrake. New York: Simon & Schuster, 1993.

Penick, Harvey. *For All Who Love the Game: Lessons and Teachings for Women*. With Bud Shrake. New York: Simon & Schuster, 1995.

Penick, Harvey. *The Game for a Lifetime: More Lessons and Teachings*. With Bud Shrake. New York: Simon & Schuster, 1996.

Penick, Harvey. *Harvey Penick's Little Red Book: Lessons and Teachings from a Lifetime in Golf*. With Bud Shrake. New York: Simon & Schuster, 1992.

Penick, Harvey. *The Wisdom of Harvey Penick: Lessons and Thoughts from the Collected Writings of Golf's Best-Loved Teacher*. With Bud Shrake. New York: Simon and Schuster, 1997.

Puckett, Earl, ed. *495 Golf Lessons by Arnold Palmer*. Northfield, IL: DBI Books, 1973.

Snead, Sam. *Golf Begins at Forty: How to Use Your Age Advantage*. With Dick Aultman. New York: Doubleday, 1978.

Snead, "Slammin' Sam." *How to Hit a Golf Ball: From Any Sort of Lie*. Garden City, NY: Garden City Books, 1950.

Snead, Sam. *Sam Snead on Golf*. Englewood Cliffs, NJ: Prentice-Hall, 1961.

Snead, Sam. *Sam Snead Teaches You His Simple "KEY" Approach to Golf*. With Larry Sheehan. New York: Atheneum, 1975.

Snead, Sam. *The Game I Love: Wisdom, Insight, and Instruction from Golf's Greatest Player*. With Fran Pirozzolo. New York: Ballantine Books, 1997.

Watson, Tom. *Tom Watson's Getting Back to Basics*. With Nick Seitz. Trumbull, CT: Golf Digest/Pocket Books, 1992.

Watson, Tom. *Getting Up and Down: How to Save Strokes from Forty Yards and In*. With Nick Seitz. New York: Times Books, 1983. First published 1983 by Random House.

Watson, Tom. *Tom Watson's Strategic Golf*. With Nick Seitz. Trumbull, CT: Golf Digest/Pocket Books, 1993.

Watson, Tom. *The Timeless Swing*. With Nick Seitz. New York: Atria Books, 2011.

Brain

Adler, Mortimer J. *How to Think About The Great Ideas.* Peru, IL: Open Court, 2002.

Bear, Mark F., Barry W. Connors, and Michael A. Paradiso. *Neuroscience: Exploring the Brain.* 3rd ed. Baltimore: Lippincott Williams & Wilkins, 2007.

Bor, Daniel. *The Ravenous Brain: How the New Science of Consciousness Explains Our Insatiable Search for Meaning.* New York: Basic Books, 2012.

Davidson, Richard J. *The Emotional Life of Your Brain: How Its Unique Patterns Affect the Way You Think, Feel, and Live—and How You Can Change Them.* With Sharon Begley. New York: Plume, 2013.

Duhigg, Charles. *The Power of Habit: Why We Do What We Do in Life and Business.* New York: Random House, 2014.

Eagleman, David. *Incognito: The Secret Lives of the Brain.* New York: Pantheon, 2011.

Fairbrother, Jeffrey T. *Fundamentals of Motor Behavior.* Champaign, IL: Human Kinetics, 2010.

Howard, Pierce J. *The Owner's Manual for The Brain: Everyday Applications from Mind-Brain Research.* 3rd ed. Austin, TX: Bard Press, 2006.

Kean, Sam. *The Tale Of The Dueling Neurosurgeons: The History of the Haman Brain as Revealed by True Stories of Trauma, Madness, and Recovery.* New York: Back Bay Books/ Little, Brown, 2014.

Medina, John. *Brain Rules: 12 Principles for Surviving and Thriving at Work, Home, and School.* Seattle: Pear Press, 2008.

Ratey, John J. *A User's Guide to the Brain: Perception, Attention, and the Four Theaters of the Brain.* New York: Vintage Books, 2002. First published in 2001 by Pantheon.

Sousa, David A. *How the Brain Learns.* 4th ed. Thousand Oaks, CA: Corwin, 2011.

Sternberg, Eliezer J. *NeuroLogic: The Brain's Hidden Rationale Behind Our Irrational Behavior.* New York: Vintage Books, 2015.

Index

Index

Index

About the Author

One of only 475 master teachers of the United States Golf Teachers Federation, Bob Mullen has played golf since he was nine years old and taught for the past twenty years.

Always an athlete, Mullen earned eight varsity letters in college; he continues to stay in shape so he can, in his seventh decade, periodically challenge Colorado's fourteeners. Immediately after college he went into the Marine Corps and was highly decorated for his service in Vietnam as a second lieutenant.

After a successful career in the plastics business, he dealt head on with his post-traumatic stress disorder by learning how the brain processes and retains information. His learning that the brain is plastic and capable of making changes throughout life led him to teach golf in a whole new way—his focus in this new book is on how the brain learns and what we can do as we practice to assist the brain in its effort to achieve our best game possible. He teaches privately in Wichita, Kansas.

Made in the USA
Middletown, DE
26 May 2020